Secrets
to
Success
for
Beginning
Elementary
School Teachers

Secrets
to
Success
for
Beginning
Elementary
School Teachers

Ellen Kottler
Nancy P. Gallavan

Skyhorse Publishing, Inc.

First Skyhorse Publishing edition 2018

Skyhorse Publishing books may be purchased in bulk at special discounts for sales promotion, corporate gifts, fund-raising, or educational purposes. Special editions can also be created to specifications. For details, contact the Special Sales Department, Sky Pony Press, 307 West 36th Street, 11th Floor, New York, NY 10018 or info@skyhorsepublishing.com.

Skyhorse® and Skyhorse Publishing® are registered trademark of Skyhorse Publishing, Inc.®, a Delaware corporation.

Visit our website at www.skyhorsepublishing.com.

10 9 8 7 6 5 4 3 2 1

Library of Congress Cataloging-in-Publication Data is available on file.

Cover design by Michael Dubowe

Print ISBN: 978-1-51073-302-2
Ebook ISBN: 978-1-51073-308-4

Printed in the United States of America

Contents

Preface

How incredibly exciting yet unbelievable! You have been given the key to your new classroom; the day has finally arrived for you to unlock the door to the place you're going to know, love, and spend as much time as you do your own home. Soon you will be immersed in attending school meetings, preparing the teaching and learning, and welcoming your elementary school students. Your teaching career is beginning at last!

There is much for you to know and remember. The details may seem insurmountable. But you can do it! Most likely, you will share this journey with many other new teachers. Only you have this book, which offers many keen insights and secrets, gathered from all kinds of first year and veteran teachers, to enhance your efficiency and strengthen your effectiveness in everything you do.

As you begin your teaching career, you have the freedom to become the educator you always dreamed of being, one who will make a difference. Consider all the possibilities you can and will create! You will establish a warm and caring learning environment; you will develop and implement challenging and engaging lesson plans. You will collaborate with all kinds of professionals and parents who want you and your students to do well. Finally, you will start earning money doing something you hope you will truly love.

You will be responsible for molding impressionable minds in positive directions. You will create the kind of dynamic classroom that you always wanted as a student—a place where real learning takes place, where everyone has fun, where there is order and support, where differences are honored yet everyone works together as a team.

OVERVIEW

This book is intended to serve as one of your mentors, a handbook that you can consult to prepare yourself for any of the usual challenges you are likely to face. It has been written specifically to reflect the realities of what most typically leads to success for beginning teachers.

We have brought together the most practical elements from the education literature and our experience. We added the advice of teachers and the wisdom of young learners (whose names are changed for privacy) to provide you with guidance during your first professional teaching position. The book includes a plethora of tips and suggestions . . . secrets that experienced teachers have discovered to simplify, organize, and reduce the stress associated with the first year on the job. Many guidelines are illustrated with vignettes that show how they can be applied in action.

CONTENTS

Secrets to Success for Beginning Elementary School Teachers has been written to assure your success in the classroom. The book's short, focused chapters address several important topics that are absolutely critical for beginning teachers. They serve as checklists for you to follow as you begin your career. Chapters 1 and 2 describe all kinds of details that you need to consider before you start teaching; we provide insights vital for learning your way around the school and organizing your classroom. Chapter 3 helps you get to know your students.

Chapters 4 through 9 systematically walk you through the first day of school and tell you how to launch effective ways to facilitate teaching and learning to meet the needs and interests of your students. Guidelines include developing meaningful curriculum, planning instruction and assessment, establishing routines and classroom management, valuing diversity, and using instructional technology. Each of these chapters reveals one valuable secret to success after another, many of which some teachers only understand, apply, or appreciate after many years of trial and error.

Chapter 10 looks at the importance of professionalism from dressing for success and maintaining confidentialities to managing time and working well with colleagues. Chapter 11 describes the pragmatic realities of building relationships with students, understanding their behaviors, and implementing classroom management strategies. Chapter 12 explores creating and maintaining positive relationships with parents or other guardians.

Then, Chapter 13 and 14 address preparing for and using substitutes, getting involved in the school, and networking with professionals. Finally, the Reflection chapter encourages you to be the teacher you want to be.

Being a teacher encompasses far more than what you do with students in your classroom. *Secrets to Success for Beginning Elementary School Teachers* reveals what you need as you progress through your first year and look ahead to many more years to come. We suggest you read the entire book both before you begin and again during the year. You'll be amazed at all there is to know and do; every day brings new challenges and rewards, and we are here to make the journey smoother for you.

As you read this book, take time to incorporate the ideas, relating them to your own classroom and students. Your geographic locations and student populations may differ, but you will benefit from the ideas we share with you. We have gathered our suggestions from many different successful teachers who want you to profit from all that they have learned much more slowly and painstakingly along the way. We want to prepare you for changes, soften the challenges, and broaden your choices as you go through your first year.

AUDIENCE

This book is written for new teachers, teachers returning to the classroom, and experienced practicing teachers mentoring new teachers or student teachers and interns, as well as for preservice teachers in the midst of their education and preparation. Each chapter presents a list of suggested activities to extend your thinking and to help you apply, within your particular classroom and situation, the ideas presented. Although the suggestions and structures we offer are based in research and practice, our intent is to be practical above all else. We provide you with all the little (and not so little) secrets that will help you to do your job in such a way that you make your classrooms fun, interesting, and satisfying—not only for your students but for yourself. Because, if you are not having fun working as a teacher, you're probably not doing it right. We want you to experience success from the very beginning!

Acknowledgments

The authors would like to thank their colleagues, students, teachers, and the young learners who contributed their insights and inspiration. Ellen thanks her husband Jeffrey, her son Cary, and her mother Fay. Nancy heartily thanks her husband Richard for his encouraging interest and care, along with her colleague LeAnn and friend Larry, for their enlightening classroom experiences and memories.

The authors would like to acknowledge the Corwin Press professionals Rachel Livsey, who suggested this book, and Phyllis Cappello for their continual support.

The contributions of the following reviewers are gratefully acknowledged:

Miranda Moe
Kindergarten Teacher/New Teacher Facilitator
South Beaver Dam Elementary School
Beaver Dam, WI

Denise Leonard
Beginning Teacher Support and Assessment (BTSA)
Staff Development Resource Teacher
Torrance, CA

Lori L. Grossman
Instructional Coordinator
Professional Development Services
Houston Independent School District
Houston, TX

About the Authors

Ellen Kottler received her bachelor's degree from the University of Michigan, her master's degree from Eastern Michigan University, and her EdS from the University of Nevada, Las Vegas. She was a secondary school teacher for over 25 years in public, private, and alternative school settings. She also served as an administrative specialist in curriculum and professional development for the Clark County School District (Las Vegas, Nevada). She is active in the National Council for the Social Studies. She is author or coauthor of several books for educators, including *On Being a Teacher: The Human Dimension* (2005), *Children With Limited English: Teaching Strategies for the Regular Classroom* (2002), and *Counseling Skills for Teachers* (2000, revised in 2007).

Ellen is currently a lecturer in the College of Education at California State University, Fullerton, and a grant writer for the Anaheim Union High School District (Anaheim, California).

Nancy P. Gallavan worked as an elementary and middle school teacher in the St. Vrain Valley and Cherry Creek School Districts of Colorado for 20 years while earning her master's degree from the University of Colorado and her PhD from the University of Denver. Prior to her current position, she was an associate professor of teacher education specializing in social studies and multicultural education at the University of Nevada, Las Vegas. Nancy has authored more than 50 publications including books, chapters, and

articles in professional education journals and is active in the
Association of Teacher Education (ATE), the National Association
for Multicultural Education (NAME), and the National Council for
the Social Studies (NCSS).

Nancy is currently Associate Dean of the College of Education
at the University of Central Arkansas in Conway, Arkansas.

CHAPTER ONE

Learning Your Way Around the School

"Welcome Visitors! Please report to the Principal's Office," reads the sign at the entrance to the elementary school. Indeed, in many ways, you are much like a visitor during your first year of teaching. You will encounter all the accompanying levels of confusion and disorientation along with the newness and excitement that are typical for an intrepid explorer who is navigating unknown territory without a map. There is much to experience and learn ahead of you, and, like the explorer, you are eager to start your journey.

As many times as you may have previously visited a school, during university field placements or perhaps even as a parent or a relative of a student, you are always struck by how big the place feels and how busy people appear to be. They all seem to know just where they are going, always in a hurry, making contact with many differ-ent people along the way. The place appears to be a maze of offices, rooms, hallways, and labs, each connected by a layout that probably once made sense to someone in charge of designing spaces. To the newcomer, however, whether an entering student or a new teacher, the school may seem overwhelming. You can't wait to start exploring!

ORIENT YOURSELF

Your first task is to learn your way around the school. We don't mean just memorizing the quickest route from the entrance to your classroom. After you've received the official tour, found out where to park, and learned what room you are assigned, make it a priority to get "unofficial" guided tours from an experienced teacher, a secretary, a student, and a custodian (especially a custodian!). This school is the place you will be spending most of your life during the coming years, so you will want to orient yourself as quickly and comprehensively as you can.

As you walk around, note how the activities of the building are organized, and start making a mental map. For example, are grade levels grouped together with K–2 in one area and 3–5 in another? Are the cafeteria and gym close to one another? Once you are settled in your classroom, you will want to locate many other important places. These include the

- principal's office(s),
- nurse's and health office,
- custodians' office,
- counselors' office(s),
- cafeteria,
- teachers' lounge,
- grade level office/workroom,
- library/media center,
- technology/computer lab,
- graphic arts and copy room,
- gym, and
- restrooms!

You want not only to find these locations but also to start learning how people operate on a daily or usual basis. Are you expected to stay on one side of the counter in the main office? Can you go into the copy room and use it when you want, or do you need to fill out a request form and submit it ahead of time? Do people use separate stairwells for going up to the second floor and coming down to the first floor? Is there a restroom specifically for adults? Who can use the small restroom in the nurse's office? How can you borrow a broom to clean up from time to time? There will be many customs to learn quickly so you understand how your new school functions and how people expect you to blend in with them (Cattani, 2002).

MAKE FRIENDS WITH THE
SECRETARIES AND ASSISTANTS

The school secretaries and administrative assistants will most likely be your first points of contact. They will help you get settled, provide you with keys and supplies, introduce you to people, and guide you through the appropriate paperwork. Spend some time getting to know the secretaries and administrative assistants as soon as you can. Ultimately, they can be your strongest supporters or the biggest obstacles throughout your career.

Most schools have teaching assistants assigned to various areas throughout the school. Every grade level may have a teaching assistant, or grade levels may share an assistant. Usually the primary grades, especially the kindergarten classrooms, have teaching assistants in every classroom. The library/media center and the technology lab probably have teaching assistants too. These individuals can help you obtain information or gain access to materials and supplies located in their areas. And although there may seem to be an abundance of individuals to get to know throughout the building, you will know who everyone is and what they do quite soon.

As you first tour the school, no doubt you will have many questions to discuss with your school guide. Rather than overwhelming this person with the sheer number of inquiries swirling around inside your head, select the most critical ones, and save the rest to ask other people later. Here is a sampling of the most critical questions that teachers need to have answered:

- What's my schedule?
- Where is the restroom?
- Where are the textbooks and supplies located?
- When's lunch?
- When do we get our class lists?
- When's the first faculty meeting?

Although all questions are important, it is vital to consider the timing of your questions. While most people are only too happy to help, be respectful of when and how often you approach them.

LEARN THE POLICIES AND REGULATIONS

You probably will be given a map of the school and an official *Teacher's Handbook* that tells you about the policies, rules, and professional responsibilities of your job. In it you will find

- the district and school mission statements;
- organizational charts;
- professional expectations for teachers;
- guidelines for teaching about controversial issues;
- selection lists of supplementary materials;
- information on the uses of technology;
- procedures for reporting child abuse;
- policies related to grading and attendance; and
- procedures regarding student discipline, safe schools, and other issues.

Read the manual carefully as soon as you get the chance, as it will include much information useful throughout the school year and your career. Here's a basic insight: the manual will answer many of your initial questions and will prevent you from looking somewhat silly if you ask them of secretaries and colleagues. Frequently, faculty meeting discussions and decisions will reference information found in the manual that everyone else already knows. You want to be well informed in preparation for these meetings, especially at the beginning of the school year.

The handbook may contain the publicly espoused values and expectations, but it does not necessarily describe how the school operates. To find out the "actual" version of the school culture (Schein, 1985), you will need to be aware of the interactions among students, staff, and faculty over time. You will want to discover answers to the following key questions:

- Who has power and control in the school?
- Who and what influences the principal most?
- How are decisions made?
- What are the major conflicts that erupt most consistently?
- What coalitions have formed among faculty and staff, and on what basis do these groups maintain their memberships?

These are just a few questions to consider. More topics will be suggested later.

PREVIEW THE DAILY AND WEEKLY SCHEDULES

Every elementary school has developed finely tuned weekly and daily schedules to ensure that all students are in school the number of minutes required by state law and receive the required number of minutes of instruction as determined for specific subject areas. Time in school includes classroom instruction as well as time for music, art, and physical education, usually called "specials." If the school has bells, they generally ring only at the beginning and the end of the school day. The teacher must be aware of the specials schedules along with times for recesses and lunch.

Schedules distributed by the principal at the first faculty meeting (or at a day-long retreat) will inform you of the days and times to be followed throughout the school. You will find out the times your students report to and are dismissed from school as well as the days and times for specials (music, art, physical education or PE, library, and perhaps technology), lunch, and recesses. Plus, you will discover if you need to meet your students in specific locations and if you are expected to escort them to and from their specials classes. You will also learn if you need to stay with your students when they are served lunch and if you have supervision "duty." And, you will learn your lunch options—the school cafeteria, the teachers' lounge, or, if there is an open campus, the places where groups go out for a quick meal.

It is helpful to know the schedules for your own students and the other classes in your grade level, as well as the schedules assigned to all other grade levels. Some schools stagger the times by grade level or even by classes within a grade level, particularly in the lunch room or on the playground (so everyone is not arriving or leaving at the same time). In addition, you (a student or a parent) may need to locate a teacher or student in another class or grade level, so we suggest that you keep one copy of the school's daily and weekly schedules handy in a notebook and another one posted on your own bulletin board for easy reference.

MEET YOUR GRADE LEVEL COLLEAGUES

Most elementary schools are organized by grade levels. If you are the single teacher in an area such as music, you may be grouped with other disciplines or specials. Many schools have designated grade level and discipline area team leaders or chairs. While their authority varies from school to school, chairs tend to serve as liaisons between the administration and the grade level faculty and staff. In some districts, the chairs are responsible for overseeing schedules and budgets; in other districts, these tasks remain the domain of the principals. Your grade level chair most likely will provide you with teacher resource materials and curriculum guides; the chair will inform you how to obtain texts for your students, supplementary materials for your teaching, and supplies for your classroom.

In some districts, the faculty members in each grade level conduct all planning together. They write lesson plans, design integrated units of learning, develop unit assessments and testing, and plan special events as a group. They meet regularly to review objectives and to discuss student progress. Most likely, you will find much-needed support and many creative ideas readily available at these meetings if this is your situation. If not, you will need to find a mentor, preferably someone who has taught your assigned grade level before and who is willing to share his or her expertise and resources with you. If such support is not available in your school, hopefully you will be able to network at district level meetings and professional conferences. In some schools, principals assign mentors formally; in other schools, you will need to seek your own avenues of support.

From a first-year teacher . . .

> I was just 21 and a new college graduate when I was hired to teach third grade at an elementary school with 920 children. Our third grade pod was located apart from the main section of the school. I had never been in this particular school, and I felt lost in every way. Fortunately, my classroom had a side door that opened into Sharon's classroom. On that first day, I introduced myself, and Sharon took me under her wing. She taught me how to make the learning both fun and productive, how to collaborate with the other third grade teachers to tap each one's expertise, and how to develop my own style. Most of all, from Sharon I learned how to pace myself so I could enjoy my work and myself to the fullest.

INSPECT YOUR CLASSROOM

Once you have been escorted to your assigned classroom and are on your own, allow yourself sufficient time to revel in the feelings that you are experiencing. This classroom is *your* room: the place where you will be working your magic. There are bulletin boards to decorate, furniture to rearrange, supplies to order and store. Mostly, though, you just want to get a feel for the space.

This classroom will become a home away from home not just for you but for your students as well. Soon you will be transforming it from four bare walls to a world of teaching and learning that is safe, welcoming, and exciting to everyone.

We suggest that you draw a map of your classroom. Note the locations of the doors, windows, permanent storage units, wallboards, and electrical outlets—items you cannot move. Include the dimensions on your map. Over the next few months, weeks, or days, you will begin to create a sense of place. You will want to carry your map with you as you select classroom supplies and decorations, and having the dimensions will be useful information. The next chapter will discuss in depth the organizing of your room.

INTRODUCE YOURSELF TO THE CUSTODIANS

Other important persons to get to know are the custodians. Most elementary schools have both a day custodian and a night custodian. The day custodian will play an important role in your life. There will be many times when you will want the day custodian to help you. You may need help moving furniture, boxes, or equipment. The day custodian will unlock your door (when you forget your key), repair the pencil sharpener, replace lights, and attend to toilets. More important, the day custodian will come to your rescue when a child is sick in your classroom. These unpredictable moments will occur, and you will need help . . . immediately. We all greatly appreciate the day custodians in every elementary school!

In the afternoon or evening, your room will be serviced by the evening custodian. While a thorough cleaning may take place once a week or less often, most likely wastebaskets will be emptied daily. Show students how to stack their chairs on their desks or tables to facilitate sweeping or vacuuming. Custodians will appreciate your keeping the room neat and having students clean up the areas where they work. Usually custodians can provide you with cleaning supplies—paper towels for unexpected spills and all-purpose cleaners for desktops. Make sure you communicate clearly the status of information left on your chalk- or whiteboards. Writing "Please do not erase; thank you!" on sections of the boards you want to keep posted will avoid miscommunication problems.

FAMILIARIZE YOURSELF WITH SAFETY

As part of your school orientation, you will need to familiarize yourself with safety procedures in the event of an emergency: fire for certain, and depending on your location, hurricanes, floods, tornadoes, earthquakes, tsunamis, landslides, or volcanic eruptions. (According to a sign posted in a New Zealand school, in the event of a volcanic eruption, you should close all windows and doors.)

In learning your way around the school, make sure to find out where the fire alarm nearest your room is located, where to direct students in the event of fires and fire drills, and where the designated shelters and supplies are for other disasters. Fire drills are usually a surprise, so be prepared. And, traditionally, one is held during the first few weeks of school.

Schools today also provide for safety and shelter-in-place protection. Your school district may have a system that uses color codes for (1) evacuating to the playgrounds, (2) securing the perimeter with activities continuing, (3) remaining in classrooms with doors locked, and (4) returning to all clear. We suggest that you tag specific pages in your school handbook with bookmarks or sticky notes for quick reference. In many schools, teachers are expected to post safety procedures; you could have these procedures and an up-to-date student roster ready on a clipboard with an attached pencil to take with you quickly in the event of relocation.

You are responsible for your students' safety as soon as they arrive on the school grounds. Systems will be in place for them to get off their school buses or out of their family cars and to walk onto the school grounds safely. There may be bus loading zones, car delivery areas, and crosswalks—all with supervision. Some elementary schools expect the teachers or teaching assistants to provide the supervision before and after school. Some elementary schools enlist the help of parent and community volunteers along with student safety patrols.

Student safety is your responsibility throughout the day. You will be informed if students have special physical, mental, or emotional needs that you must attend to during both formal and informal instructional times. You may be required to meet a particular student at the door each morning and provide assistance. You will be informed of students who take medications, and you will be responsible for seeing that students not only deliver their medications to the nurse in the health office but also go to the nurse in the health office at the specified times to take the prescribed medications. Plus, you will be told about students who have estranged family members whom they cannot see or with whom they cannot leave school at any time. Keep a record of this information as you get it. We suggest a notebook that you can carry with you.

Check your handbook for your responsibilities as a teacher. You will probably discover that your responsibility for the students in your care continues should an emergency extend beyond the school day. You will want to talk with your students about procedures if they get home and no one is there. Many students live within walking distance of the school; they may return to you or the main office for assistance.

Although students' telephone numbers and addresses are kept in the main office, we suggest that you create a directory of your own, listing this information along with work locations, telephone numbers, and e-mail addresses for the parents; the grade levels and teachers' names of siblings; and any other pertinent information that you may want at your fingertips, especially when the main office is closed. One teacher we know keeps a notebook with her at all times throughout the school year, so she can reach her students and their families whenever necessary.

Also, you are responsible for your own safety and that of your family. If you have an elderly parent or young children of your own for whom you provide care, develop contingency plans for them. Think about how your family members will be cared for on those days that you need to go to work early or stay late. Some of these extended days will be planned, and you can make arrangements in advance; others will be unplanned. Establish ways that you and your family can communicate easily about times when your plans change unexpectedly—such as when you need to attend an emergency faculty meeting or parent conference after school. And try to arrange this communication so it doesn't disturb your professional duties.

Also, sometimes you will elect to stay late to work on a special project in your classroom. Please do not stay at your school all alone if your principals and colleagues have urged you to leave when they leave. You always want to let someone in the office know your plans, and you want to tell the evening custodian too. No one wants to be surprised by the other.

INVESTIGATE YOUR SCHOOL'S TRADITIONS

Every school has its own unique culture and customs. Some customs are established by the administration, such as dress codes; others emerge from student, staff, faculty, or parent input, such as school mascots and school colors. Back-to-School Night, Open House, parent-teacher conferences, curriculum fairs, award ceremonies, holiday celebrations, fundraisers and other events often have many rituals associated with them. For example, November may be marked by food drives held around Thanksgiving.

Some schools also collect blankets and toiletries to distribute to the homeless. National Education Week is celebrated the third week in November with recognition for teachers that may range from school banners to small gifts of appreciation from students, the school, the district, or parent organizations. Throughout the year, there will be school assemblies for different purposes, such as guest speakers and awards for student achievements. Most likely, there will be grade level programs along with choir, orchestra, and band concerts in the evenings along with schoolwide festivals and schoolwide dances.

These traditions are as much a part of the school experience as anything to do with the physical building. They may sound a bit confusing, if not overwhelming. The point is that you fully join the school culture, becoming part of the school family. Students and administration will greatly appreciate your visible support and eager participation.

ACQUAINT YOURSELF WITH THE SCHOOL'S HISTORY

Your elementary school may have a long and rich history. Perhaps you attended this school as an elementary school student yourself, and returning as a teacher is a dream come true. You'll be amazed at the number of people who stop by after school or attend the special events to see their old classrooms and past teachers. Soon you will be one of these past teachers sharing memories with your previous students.

Find out more about your school's history. Perhaps the school is named for a city or state leader. Ask who your notable alumni are. Here's a story illustrative of this insight from a new teacher:

> I was zipping along through my teaching day in mid-September during my first year of teaching. The door opened and there stood the principal and the state governor. No one had warned me that either one of them was coming. Fortunately, the classroom was in good order; the students were engaged in writing autobiographies and drawing self-portraits for display at the upcoming Back-to-School Night. The principal walked over to me and introduced the governor. As a young child, the governor and his family had lived in the neighborhood and attended my school! He was holding a press conference later that day to promote increasing funds for education and wanted to see his former classroom.
>
> The principal introduced the governor to the fourth graders, telling the students why the governor wanted to visit the school and this particular classroom. The students were great. We had just started studying state history in social studies, so we knew where the state capital is located, who the governor is, and some of his duties. The governor allowed them to ask him some questions. Plus, I had placed the students' names on their desks, so the governor could call on individuals by name. Impressive!
>
> Fortunately, I had brought an inexpensive camera to school to keep in my desk for moments just like this. I asked the governor's assistant if I could take photographs of the governor with my students. This was approved, so all the students got their pictures taken with the governor. Those students will always remember the day the governor came to visit. Most of all, we were all in awe that a fourth grader who sat in our room, grew up to become the leader of our state!

INTRODUCE YOURSELF TO OTHERS

As you cross paths with other people, introduce yourself and tell them what you teach. This is how you will build important relationships with the school personnel. When you talk to others, remind them of your name. We offer two secrets to help you learn new names and faces. First, get a copy of the previous year's school pictures, yearbook, or newsletters. Here you will see the teachers for each grade level and area of specialization, the teaching assistants, the principals, and the administrative assistants. You can read about various events featured by grade levels or areas of specialization, about afterschool clubs, and about the traditional activities anticipated eagerly by students, their families, and the community.

Second, sit next to a friendly colleague or your mentor at faculty meetings and ask that person to quietly identify a few individuals at each meeting. Faculty and staff tend to sit at meetings with other members of their grade level teams or teaching groups. Individuals tend to speak for their whole group when expressing an opinion. New teachers can rapidly associate members of various groups with their voiced concerns.

Be assured you won't remember all the names of people the first time you meet them, nor will they remember yours. You will have to ask individuals again to tell you their names and what they do. You may not remember where everything is located either. It takes time to learn your way around the school.

TAKE A BREATH . . .

The first year of teaching is indeed one of the most exhilarating and challenging times in your career (Kottler, Zehm, & Kottler, 2005). Remember that it will happen to you only once; yet this remarkable experience will remain with you for the rest of your life. You will be tested in ways that you can't imagine, and you will find rewards in the most unanticipated moments. You will learn many things about yourself and the process of learning.

There will be precious little time for contemplation or in-depth planning. Your time will be taken up by meetings, grading, and trying to stay ahead of the students. Some of the things you hope to do will be put aside, at least temporarily. That's okay. Your main job is just to learn your way around, to get to know your students, and to experiment with teaching styles and methods until you find things that work well for you and your students. As you find time, you can reacquaint yourself with some of the classic literature (Bruner, 1977; Dewey, 1938), university textbooks (Wink, 2004; Zimmermann & Keene, 1997), and supplementary guides to help you with the first days of school (Jones, 2000; Wong & Wong, 2001). Before you know it, you will be the expert showing someone else around the new school.

Suggested Activities

1. Next time you are in an elementary school, note the school layout and the traffic patterns both inside and around the outside of the school. Discuss how the school is organized so it runs smoothly and meets various functions. Examine the before- and afterschool activities.

2. Shadow a teacher for a day. Note where the teacher goes and how many people the teacher comes in contact with during a given day.

3. Find out what names you should use to address the secretaries, teaching assistants, custodians, cafeteria workers, and other staff members. Find out what names your students should use. In some schools, everyone uses a title and last name to address everyone all the time. In other schools, adults use their first names in private conversations.

4. Make a copy of the fire and other designated safety procedures right away so you know where to go at all times whether you are with students or not with students.

CHAPTER TWO

Organizing Your Classroom

Once you can find your way around the school, the next priority is to organize the personal space in which you will be operating. The impression the room gives as the students (and their parents and principals) enter will set the tone for your class (Cattani, 2002). You know from your own experiences as a student that there exists quite a different atmosphere in a room that seems drab and uninviting versus one that positively vibrates with energy. You also know that different things happen in a room that is arranged with desks in neat rows versus rooms arranged with desks in small groups. If you establish cooperative learning routines with the students, desks can quickly be arranged and rearranged throughout the school day (Johnson & Johnson, 1999; Slavin, 1995). Consider not only how desks are arranged, but think how whiteboards, blackboards, and bulletin boards will be utilized, as well as how desk, table, bookshelf, and cabinet space will be used.

> "I like it when the desks are placed in groups of four or five desks. I like working with other people and getting to know new people."
>
> —Madison, age 11, Grade 5

The culture of your school, what other teachers are doing around you, the subjects you are teaching, and your personal philosophy of learning will each contribute to the goals you have for organizing your classroom. As you begin to set up your classroom, consider the needs of your students as well as your own. We hope you will experiment with alternative classroom designs and express your unique style through your teaching.

SURVEY YOUR SPACE

The first step in organizing your room is to examine the resources you have. Spend a few minutes sitting in different parts of the room to observe what it feels like. Where is the flag located? Where are the intercom speaker and controls placed? Where are the supply closets, cabinets, and bookshelves situated? Imagine you are a student sitting there, daydreaming about something important rather than paying attention to whatever is going on in the room at the time. Check what is within the visual field from each point in the room. How is the lighting? Listen for the acoustics as well, to hear how sound travels, both for sounds within the classroom and for potentially distracting noises outside. Also, note what type of heating or air conditioning system is used. Will students be subjected to strong air blowing on them depending on where they sit? Notice how the features of the room will affect students.

Survey where the bulletin boards and chalkboards or whiteboards are located, as well as the pencil sharpeners, lights, electric sockets, overhead projector, computer, or any other available equipment. Remember, when you use any audiovisual aids, you will need access to electricity and ways to avoid glare so the screens are clearly visible. If you have a telephone line in your room, you will want to position a table and chair or desk near the phone jack.

Next, look at the furniture and equipment that have been placed in your classroom. Do you have bookshelves, tables, chairs, desks, student storage spaces, file cabinets, a wardrobe, a computer? Is there any audiovisual equipment in the room? What items do you feel are most important? For now, make a list of what you need, and hold onto it until you figure out the most politically expedient ways to lobby for what you want. And if, for example, you are lacking computer technology in the classroom, find out how to reserve time in computer labs or in the library for student projects and teacher preparation.

Most schools have a media or audiovisual center where equipment is stored. Sometimes equipment is kept in a central storage area of the school or within the grade level office space. Even if you don't have permanent equipment, you might be able to gain access to things on an as-needed basis or share with another teacher. In addition, many districts have media centers offering a wide variety of instructional materials available for teachers to reserve and use. Be aware that in some states the resources are housed at regional rather than district levels.

We know teachers spend much of their own money on their classrooms and students. Here's an important tip: keep the receipts of your personal expenditures on school materials to use for income tax deductions. Plus, you can find all kinds of discounted, inexpensive, or free resources, materials, and furniture at yard and garage sales, thrift stores, public libraries, local bookstores, craft and material stores, public organizations and institutions, and tourist centers, or through want ads and book-order clubs. With time, your collection of resources will grow!

ESTABLISH PLACEMENT AND MOVEMENT

Room arrangement is critical to maintaining student safety as well as engaging students actively in various class functions. From what direction will the students enter the room? Will they have sufficient space to walk by desks or tables with their big backpacks and book bags? You have probably already considered how you want to arrange the room to fit your teaching style and course content. Will students be listening most of the time, working in small groups in special areas, or studying with partners at desks? Will students need to move around to engage in cooperative group work? Will students need access to resources or reference materials? And how will you move around the room to help and monitor student progress when students are working individually, in groups, or as a whole class?

> "Most teachers put the desks in rows; one teacher put the desks in a horseshoe. I liked the horseshoe. I could see without anything getting in my way. I like it when they move the desks around and I sit in different places too!"
>
> —Riley, age 9, Grade 3

Specific seating arrangements are designed to accomplish different goals. As you walk around the school visiting other teachers, check out the ways they have arranged their rooms. Note the advantages and disadvantages of each arrangement. Common configurations include

- traditional rows of desks to maximize the number of students in the room and maintain order;
- rows of desks facing each other across a center divide to encourage student-teacher interaction;
- horseshoe arrangement with desks facing the front for maximum eye contact with students;
- tables seating small groups of four to six students for cooperative learning;
- desks in one large circle to facilitate student interaction; and
- a "fishbowl" design, with an inner and outer circle of desks.

Of course, a combination of arrangements may be possible, depending on the particular learning activity. One way to keep students engaged is to devise ways that move them around from one seating arrangement to another. Nevertheless, you will still want to settle on one stable arrangement to begin with, at least to facilitate taking attendance until you get to know the students. Later, you can practice having students select a seating plan so they can rearrange their seats quickly and quietly.

> "I like it really fun with lots of designs."
>
> —Vanessa, age 7, Grade 1

One other consideration in space design is related to managing students' behaviors. You will want to make sure to arrange things in such a way that allows you full view of everything going on in the room. When teaching groups or the whole class, many teachers prefer to use an overhead projector, so they can face the students rather than turn their backs and write on the front board. You want to be aware of where you place bookshelves or dividers; you should be able to see all parts of the room from your desk and work areas. Also, you will want to consider potential problems that could emerge. If you don't want students to cross your line of vision during your instruction, place the objects they need to access, such as boxes of tissue, baskets of paper, pencil sharpeners, and wastebaskets, at strategic points on the sides of the room. Here are some secrets to success: putting a wastebasket near the pencil sharpener will help you and your students keep that area clean, and acquiring an electric sharpener or two will cause students to spend less time at the sharpener. Electric sharpeners are just as noisy as the hand-operated kind, but the use is quicker.

"I like a room that's neat, organized, nothing on the ground. And clean desks, clean room overall."

—Zachary, Age 10 (almost 11), Grade 5

ARRANGE LEARNING STATIONS AND CENTERS

Most elementary school teachers include various learning areas called stations or centers depending on whether students just pass through for an activity or spend time completing projects at tables located around the room. The learning stations and centers might include

- reading nooks with rugs and floor pillows around bookshelves;
- computer corners with scanners and printers;
- listening posts with headphones and AV equipment; and
- tables with supplies, realia, and resources for
  - writing—lined paper, pencils, dictionaries;
  - spelling—word lists, paper, pencils;
  - math—rulers, calculators, manipulatives;
  - science—lab equipment, sink, goggles;
  - social studies—maps, globes, atlases, colored pencils; and
  - art—crayons, scissors, glue, paper scraps, yarn, fabric.

Stations and centers need to be arranged so each individual or group can work quietly and independently while other students are either working with the teacher, at their desks, or at their own stations or centers. Some of the centers will be accessed at specific times by identified groups of students. If this is your situation, we suggest this helpful secret: create five centers, one for each day of the week. Divide your class into five groups so each group visits each center each week. You can change the activities at the centers once a week or once every two weeks, depending on the time students have to access the centers and the nature of the activities.

"One teacher had centers for reading, writing, math sheets, art projects, and fun stuff. We just went to the centers when we were finished with our work. I always went to the fun stuff."

—Riley, age 9, Grade 3

A new teacher shared with us . . .

I had not gone to an elementary school where centers were used; one of my university methods professors had described centers to us, and they sounded both exciting and effective. During my field placement, I was assigned to a fourth-grade teacher who rotated students through ten centers every two weeks. Centers were used to introduce new ideas, to reinforce previously learned material, and to provide outlets for students to express their creativity. Here I saw the concept in practice and decided right away that I would use them in my future classroom too. The teacher I was observing even had a student helper assist in setting up and maintaining the centers.

CONSIDER WHITEBOARDS AND BULLETIN BOARDS

One of the first things people notice when they walk into a classroom is the material displayed on the walls. You probably want information related to every part of the curriculum with a balance of manufactured and teacher created displays. Most important, you want to allocate space to display student work. Yet, the bulletin boards do not need to be completely decorated before school begins; this secret may be a surprise to you. We suggest you wait until your students arrive to finish some of the bulletin boards together. Then you and your students can add to the bulletin boards and change them together throughout the year. This approach gives your students immediate ownership of the space.

Many teachers establish a motif for decorating their classrooms, i.e., symbols, designs, or cartoon characters, which they use to help their students identify with the new space. The motif doesn't have to be fancy. Some grade level teaching teams collaborate, so everyone in a particular grade level is identified by a related design such as five different shapes, five different continents, or five different members of a cartoon ensemble.

Reflections from a first-year teacher . . .

> I dedicated specific bulletin boards to specific purposes. For example, the bulletin board near the door displayed organizational and safety information. Bulletin boards on all the walls displayed information and items related to the various learning centers. The long bulletin board along the wall under the windows had a clip for each student to display stories, drawings, and other work. I kept the floor space near this bulletin board open, and encouraged students to go read one another's postings. I tried to keep the bulletin board displays neat and to a minimum, so they were not too distracting.
>
> When I began teaching, I thought I was responsible for all of the bulletin board displays and that they should be assembled before the students started school. I soon learned that, to build a more cohesive community of learners, the students could (and should) help construct the displays. Not only did they offer great ideas, but they wanted to do the work! I formed small committees that rotated throughout the year, so everyone got to do all sorts of jobs. What a terrific way to make the classroom "ours." I loved hearing them tell their friends from other classrooms or their parents how they helped decorate our classroom.

You need to model and reinforce appropriate respect for displayed work. Naturally, some students excel more than others, and their accomplishments might outshine those of some of the other students. You do not want to force a student who feels inadequate to display work that others will ridicule. Find a way for each student to excel and be honored among peers.

Bulletin boards are useful for brightening up the room as well as helping you to emphasize key points of given lessons. As part of a social studies lesson, you would expect to see pictures of past achievements. For English or language arts, you might see rules to use for writing or pictures of famous authors and samples of their works. For mathematics, you might post geometric patterns, new terminology, or famous mathematicians' portraits. But these are only traditional applications; you can be much more creative!

As noted in the example above, most teachers post the daily schedule and assignments, along with other school- or district-mandated announcements, such as the school mission statement and where to go for a fire drill. You may choose to use some of the space to display material on current events. Most teachers use some space to display student work, turning their classrooms into museum galleries by the end of the year with exhibitions of student-created artifacts and projects.

In deciding what to do with your bulletin boards, consider the following functions to engage students (Edwards, Gandani, & Forman, 1998):

- Informative—giving facts,
- Rule giving—providing guidelines,
- Demonstrative—showing examples,
- Motivational—promoting inspiration,
- Stimulating—posing questions or new ideas,
- Rewarding—displaying student work,
- Aesthetic—reflecting interests and likes,
- Reinforcing—offering support, and
- Entertaining—using humor.

CHECK EQUIPMENT AND STORAGE

Before you put your plan into action and start moving heavy furniture around the room, we suggest you design a blueprint on a piece of paper, positioning each piece of furniture and equipment. Consult the following checklists for items to include:

Table 2.1

Permanent Features Checklist	
___ Placement of door(s)	___ Chalk- or dry-erase boards
___ Electric sockets	___ Lighting
___ Bulletin boards	___ Telephone line
___ Light switch(es)	___ Stationary cabinets
___ Pencil sharpener(s)	___ Laboratory (science, art) equipment
___ Location of windows	___ Sinks, drinking fountains, restrooms
___ Coat hooks	

Table 2.2

Technology-related Equipment Checklist

___ Computer(s)	___ Laser disc player
___ VCR	___ Overhead projector
___ Television	___ Screen
___ Audiotape player; CD player, record player	___ Opaque projector

Table 2.3

Furniture Checklist

___ Teacher's desk and chair	___ Wastebasket(s)
___ Stool	___ File cabinet(s)
___ Podium	___ Table(s)
___ Wardrobe(s)	___ Chairs
___ Student desks or tables	___ Bookshelves

LOCATE MATERIALS AND SUPPLIES

Once the furniture is arranged, next you will need to concentrate on supplies that will be useful in your work. First, take inventory of what is already available in your classroom. Then, make a list of items you will need, based on these suggestions:

- writing implements: pens, markers, pencils, colored pencils, dry-erase markers or chalk, overhead markers;
- paper: lined paper, construction paper, plain paper, sticky (small and large) notes, file cards;
- adhesives: Scotch tape, masking tape, glue, stapler, staples, paper clips (large and small);
- storage items: file folders, hanging folders;
- tools: ruler, scissors, three-hole punch, hammer, nails, screwdriver;
- attendance book;
- planning book and calendar;
- media supplies: videotapes, computer disks;
- reference materials: atlases, dictionaries, thesauruses;
- multipurpose cleaner and paper towels;
- tissues;

- snacks to munch on (for you and the students, if allowed);
- emergency sewing kit;
- camera;
- key to the classroom; and
- keys to your desk, personal closet space, and file cabinet.

In addition to these general classroom supplies, you will also need textbooks and related materials as well as resources related to your specific content standards, such as manipulatives for math activities; chemicals for science experiments; playground equipment for outdoor play; and paint, scissors, and clay for art projects. Consult with your colleagues for suggestions in this area.

COLOR CODE MATERIALS AND EQUIPMENT

A helpful way to organize materials is to color code items for each subject area. For example, use a yellow book cover on the text, yellow file folders, and a yellow notebook binder for materials related to science, and store resources in a yellow bin—blue for math, green for social studies, and so on.

It is also wise to create a file of "emergency" enrichment or review activities that can be used at any time. You may want to color these red so they will be easy to find. They will be useful in any of the following scenarios:

1. You are called away from the class;

2. An unanticipated guest, such as a parent or a university education student, drops in for a visit taking your attention away from the class temporarily;

3. The students finish an activity more quickly than you anticipated with plenty of time before the end of the period;

4. You discover that students don't have the prior knowledge you expected in order to move to the next level activity.

POST SCHEDULES AND PROCEDURES

One area of the classroom should display weekly and daily schedules as well as procedures for both regular events as well as emergencies.

If the teacher and students know that these types of information will always be posted in this location, they can not only reference the information quickly and easily but also direct new students, parents, teaching assistants, or substitute teachers to the display to find out more about schedules and procedures. Having a designated place for the weekly and daily schedules will alert students to various upcoming special events in advance and help them to begin managing their time. Later, you can include the assignment for each subject or hang a sample product with assessment rubric. Creating an assignment board will allow students to become more responsible for knowing about their assignments, especially when they are out of the room for short periods of time or are absent. You see the importance of arranging your room so students are as independent and self-sufficient as possible.

POSITION BASKETS, FILES, AND MAILBOXES

Many elementary school teachers devise a system of work baskets or hanging files to organize resources and assignments. You might want to have a stack of baskets with classroom supplies, such as lined paper, graph paper, drawing paper, scrap paper, and blank assignment sheets. Then you might want to have a series of baskets or files for reading, spelling, writing, math, science, and social studies. Each subject area needs one basket or file to hold the assignments and one basket to hold the completed assignments. Don't forget to color code them—it helps you and your students stay organized!

We have found it extremely helpful to create a mailbox for each student. You can use recycled milk cartons, heavy-duty boxes, or cardboard ice cream buckets stapled together. A mailbox system allows you to return papers to students when they are not in the classroom and leave announcements to be taken home. If you use a homework folder system, you, the students, a teaching assistant, or a volunteer helper can collect the assignments and messages in each mailbox easily and place them in each folder before the end of the day to be taken home. You and your students need to be able to access the mailboxes readily.

SET UP YOUR DESK

Your desk houses many different items. We suggest that you purchase some metal organizers to keep on the top of your desk; you will use them throughout your career. Here you can store some of those essential items you will reference frequently, such as your daily planner, grade book, state academic standards references, substitute teacher file, and emergency information. Some teachers keep their daily planners open on their desks at all times. You may also keep pictures and decorative items on your desk. Anything else on the top of your desk most likely will be used by your students, such as pencils, staplers, paper clips, scissors, sticky notes, and tape. You will need to inform students what to do if they want or need items that are on or in your desk.

Items you want to keep for yourself, such as special pens, calculators, and computer items, you probably want to store in the top drawers. However, certain items you will need to keep private, such as students' medical information, students' test scores, class money, and your purse or backpack. Place these items in a lockable drawer of your desk, if not a lockable cupboard or closet. Do not leave confidential information or valuables out in the open.

GATHER FIRST-AID SUPPLIES

Having easy access to first-aid supplies in an elementary school classroom is a must. Band-Aids are commonly requested, and you may need to monitor their use. You will want to have the basic supplies readily available so as not to waste class time looking for them. You will probably receive Band-Aids, a disinfectant, cotton swabs, sterile gauze pads, and gloves in a first-aid kit from the nurse's or health office. It is a good idea to include safety pins in the kit for torn clothing. For serious problems, immediately refer the student to the school nurse or health aide. Most schools expect teachers to use a specific form and a hall pass to send students to the nurse.

CREATE AN INVITING SENSE OF PLACE . . .

You may decide to bring some things from home to make your classroom more comfortable or cozy, such as a fan, a desk lamp, posters, magazines and books, or special supplies. Some teachers bring in plants, stuffed animals, and comfortable chairs or sofas—district rules and space permitting. However, you will need to be sensitive to student allergies.

How you arrange the space for learning is as critical as anything else you do as part of your teaching method and style (Meager, 1996). If the learning environment is uncomfortable, unattractive, distracting, or dull, you cannot maximize the possibilities for creative fun and focused concentration that will be necessary in the tasks that you plan. Your classroom is your new home. Customize and decorate it in such a way that it becomes a comfortable base for your work and an inviting place for others to visit.

Suggested Activities

1. Walk around a school and notice all the different ways that classrooms are organized. Consider bulletin boards, furniture placement, equipment, and storage. Analyze which arrangements, in your opinion, are the most comfortable and effective for student learning.

2. Observe how teachers establish and use learning stations and centers. Identify the components of productive centers, considering locations, resources, directions, and expectations.

3. Envision where you will place your teaching resources. You may want to set up several areas so you can access materials quickly at your desk, at your reading table, near the whiteboard, or other places.

4. Consider where you will keep your personal items and your key to the classroom so you can retrieve them privately and quickly as needed.

CHAPTER THREE

Knowing Your Students

Now that you've started getting your room ready, it is time to concentrate on the young people with whom you will be working. Within a very short time, you will be exposed to a new group of students, each with unique names to pronounce correctly and individual needs and wants to address. You'll likely meet their parents or guardians, siblings, and maybe grandparents too.

GET YOUR CLASS LIST

The principal or grade level chair will give you your class list during the noninstructional day(s) before school opens or when you begin in the classroom. If time permits, review your class list with your grade level colleagues as well as with the previous grade level teachers to learn about each student. Find out how to pronounce each student's name correctly and whether there is a preferred nickname. Ask if there are any specific academic, social, or home circumstances that you need to know about before the school year begins. As you organize your classroom, obtain supplies, and prepare handouts, also put together some extra packets of introductory materials for students who might transfer into your class later during the year.

SEND A WELCOMING POSTCARD

After you get your class list, we highly recommend that you send your students a welcoming postcard. This may occur during the summer vacation, a few weeks before school starts, or merely days before the opening of the new school year. You can get plain post-cards at the post office and add a sticker previewing the theme of your classroom. Or, you can use picture postcards from the local area or from other places you have recently visited. Some places will give you postcards free or at a reduced cost if you tell them you are using them with your students. Just ask!

The space is limited, so write "Hi" and use the student's name. Get the name from school records, and, if you can, check with the previous year's teacher to be sure this is the first name that the student commonly uses. You might make an error here, but this name is all you have, and the student will like getting the post card.

Here's what one teacher writes on his postcards:

> Hi Brent! Welcome to the Third-Grade Stars! My name is Mr. Park, and I am your new teacher. School starts on Monday, August 30. Please bring this postcard to school next week. See you soon, Mr. Park.

Most of the students excitedly bring their postcards on the first day. Mr. Park reads a story about stars to the class and gives a small sheet of colorful star stickers to all students to place on their individual work folders. The theme of his classroom is stars. The students who did not receive postcards, lost their postcards, or are new to the class, also receive postcards. It is important to play fair from the very first day of school.

A sixth-grade teacher we know sends postcards with pictures from around the world. In class, she distributes world atlases that the school has purchased for each student. The students are encouraged to use the postcards as bookmarks in the atlases. On the first day of school, the teacher previews learning about the world as part of all their upcoming subject areas, tying together the classroom theme with the postcards. As a highlight, the teacher invites her friend from China to write each student's name in Chinese. It is an exciting first day of school that grabs the students' attention.

GATHER STUDENT INFORMATION

As you continue to prepare for the upcoming school year, gather some general information about the backgrounds and heritages of your students. Read each student's cumulative record and academic portfolio to become fully acquainted with each student's potential. There you may discover the special gifts or talents of students, the special programs in which they may be enrolled, and specific learning, behavioral, or medical concerns. Determine which children have Individualized Education Plans (IEPs) and how to access those plans.

Some students come to school directly from their own homes; others ride buses before and after school. Some go to day care programs before and/or after school. Students who walk to school usually stay at home with a parent or grandparent until it is close to the start of school, or they walk from a neighbor's home. These students tend to be more refreshed and ready to engage in academic schoolwork. Here are some valuable secrets to success. Students who ride buses to school usually have started their days earlier than students who walk to school. Bus rides may be quite lengthy (up to an hour one way) resulting in students who are less refreshed and less ready to engage in schoolwork.

Students who attend a before-school, public or private day care program may also have started the day quite early. Some parents must drop off their children several hours before school starts. Some elementary schools offer their own before- and afterschool day care programs. In these situations, some of your students may be spending more time at school than you are. What your students do in the early mornings before school certainly can impact their attention spans, hunger pangs, and energy levels.

During the first week of school, you can ask your students all kinds of questions either orally or in writing. You and your grade level colleagues may want to construct an information survey form for students to complete at school or with their parents at home. The information requested could include the following:

- Name and nickname
- Address
- Telephone number(s) including home, cell, and fax as appropriate (Sometimes students have their own personal home and cell telephone numbers, while others may not have any phone at home.)
- E-mail address, if appropriate
- Birthday
- Age

- Mother's or guardian's name, telephone numbers at home and work, and e-mail address
- Father's or guardian's name, telephone numbers at home and work, and e-mail address (You may also want to inquire as to what hours the parents or guardians work.)
- Names of brothers and sisters (including last names if the last names are different), their grade levels, and their teachers' names—especially for siblings attending the same elementary school
- Other family members' and friends' names, telephone numbers, and e-mail addresses that the teacher may need to have, i.e., grandparents, day care providers, etc.
- Language skills (Ask, "What is your first language?" then "What languages are spoken in the home?" and "What languages do you read?") Here you will learn if there is support in the home for English language (or foreign language) activities. Some students will not be able to get help with their homework in subjects such as English grammar if their parents or guardians do not speak English. This information will be useful as well in planning for communication with parents where translators or translations may be needed (Kottler & Kottler, 2002).
- Activities, hobbies, and interests (Ask students some of these questions: "Do you play an instrument?" "Do you play sports?" "What activities do you participate in before school? After school? Until what time?" "What are your hobbies and special interests?") Here you will learn how students spend their time outside of school.

ESTABLISH A SHARED LEARNING COMMUNITY

As you greet your students by the classroom door, say hello, shake their hands, and say their names. As you and your students become acquainted with one another, you begin to establish a shared learning community (Kriete, 2003). The difference between most classrooms and a learning community centers on the attitudes and actions of the teacher. Rather than projecting an atmosphere in which the teacher directs and the students comply, in a learning community the teacher becomes an equal member of the group. A sense of shared togetherness permeates the classroom. Everyone feels safe, welcome, and excited about school; decisions are made by everyone thinking aloud, sharing ideas, and deciding together.

Here are some guidelines to help teachers create a shared learning community:

- greet students warmly and genuinely at the door every morning and whenever students return to the classroom;
- start the day with a morning meeting discussing events related to the school and students (as well as the community, state, and nation);
- emphasize the sharing of thoughts, feelings, and actions (balancing cognitive, affective, and physical interactions);
- develop classroom "rules" or expectations collaboratively, with the teacher and students working together;
- use friendly signals (such as gentle singing or soft chimes) to realign and redirect energies;
- expect students to treat one another and themselves with kindness and respect, then model and reinforce this behavior;
- create and maintain classroom displays collaboratively based on shared needs, wants, and expectations;
- study and complete projects working with partners or in cooperative learning groups;
- incorporate creativity, playfulness, and fun into the learning;
- be sure that everyone has the necessary tools to complete every task (i.e., find ways of providing tools and of having individuals become responsible for their own tools that do not escalate into power struggles);
- take time to share outcomes and reflect upon discoveries both as new content and developing processes;
- provide genuine and pragmatic feedback to learning;
- show students authenticity in learning with them and from them;
- emphasize less telling and more sharing, with less teacher talk and more student talk;
- integrate time throughout the day to share books and to make connections among text, self, and the world in various ways; and
- allocate plenty of time before the end of the day to close the day.

LEARN YOUR STUDENTS' CULTURAL BACKGROUNDS

We're sure you've heard how important it is to become aware of the ethnic and cultural backgrounds of your students in order to interpret behavior appropriately (Oakes & Lipton, 2003). For example, some students will not ask questions when they don't understand an idea or a direction because they have been taught to not bother adults. Questioning may not be valued in their families. Students may simply tell the teacher what the teacher wants to hear—yes, they understand an assignment; yes, they can do a math problem—even when, in fact, they could use some help and reassurance.

Some cultural backgrounds of students may dictate that they are passive observers rather than active participants. One way to make sure you involve each student is to write each student's name on a popsicle-type craft stick. Keep the sticks in a can, pulling them out as you call on students to respond to questions or when you need "volunteers." Here's another secret: instruct each student who speaks in class to select the person who will talk next, indicating, however, that the student may pick only someone who has not yet participated. This ensures that no one ends up being left out. It is indeed a challenge to achieve equitable participation in class so the same loud voices do not always dominate.

Another way is to pass out index cards (or have each student take out a piece of paper) and ask students to write down a question or response to a prompt for you to address in class. This way, each person's contribution is included. You have the choice of getting students to sign their contributions or not.

Body language differs from group to group. Certain cultures teach that children should look down, averting their eyes as a sign of respect. Other cultures teach that a child should not look away but should look directly into the eyes of the person who is talking. To avoid problems of communication, the teacher must examine his or her own culture and the cultural of the students; the teacher must become aware of cultural differences when interpreting both verbal and nonverbal cues. We address cultural diversity in much greater detail in Chapter 8.

Your students may come from a variety of socioeconomic levels. Students from families with high socioeconomic status (SES) tend to have stronger academic backgrounds, show higher school performance, and have access to more resources than those with lower SES. Students from lower SES backgrounds will need more support (Flannery & Jehlen, 2005).

Elementary schools across the United States are changing rapidly. In many schools, the populations of students from Latino backgrounds and Asian origins are increasing. A growing number of U.S. students speak a language other than English at home, and many are new immigrants (Black, 2006). What this means is that, as teachers, we can no longer hold onto one reference point of expectations. There is no "dominant" culture to rely upon as a norm. Importantly, this makes for some very challenging situations that require flexible attitudes for adapting how we teach to an increasingly diverse population.

FOCUS ON GENDER EQUITY

Teachers need to provide equal opportunity for and interact equally with girls and boys. Title IX of the Education Amendments Act of 1972 guarantees equal educational opportunity and, therefore, bans discrimination based on gender. In the early 1990s, studies supported by the American Association of University Women Education Foundation (AAUWEF) examined gender differences in the classroom and showed that boys received more attention from teachers than girls, were more likely to take advanced math and science and related classes, and continued in gifted and talented programs longer than girls. Studies also showed that girls received better grades from elementary through college and that, though identified more often for gifted programs in elementary school, they did not continue in them. While later studies indicate progress in this area, gender equity continues to be a concern for all teachers (AAUWEF, 1998).

Be aware of your own background, behaviors, and biases, and your use of classroom resources. When planning activities, involve girls and boys equally, and use cooperative learning regularly. You can do this by assigning seats that have boys and girls sitting next to one another, assigning group membership rather than letting students choose their own, and calling on students rather than letting them call out answers because boys typically answer more frequently and more quickly than girls. You should follow up equally with boys and girls so both give complete answers, and you should ask complex follow-up questions of each. Plus, take some time to develop a monitoring system (like names on popsicle sticks as described above or checkmarks on a seating chart) to ensure that you call on all students equally. Find instructional materials that have female as well as male models and examples that challenge stereotypes. Encourage and praise *all* students in mathematics, science, and reading, not just those who obviously excel.

EXPLORE YOUR STUDENTS' LEARNING STYLES

Students differ in how they receive and process information, but they will have consistent response patterns. In order to promote student achievement, teachers must not only recognize and teach to each student's preferred learning style but also help students become more comfortable and accomplished at learning through all other learning styles (Armstrong, 1993). Be aware of your preferred and commonly used teaching style(s); try to use a variety of styles throughout each day and within all subject areas.

While Chapter 6 addresses planning instruction and assessment, we present a description of different kinds of learning styles here with corresponding techniques to incorporate them quickly and easily into your classroom:

Sensory Modalities. You are probably aware that students receive information through their senses. Some learn best by seeing information; these are the visual learners who process the world primarily through observation. For them, graphic organizers, charts, tables, pictures, and videos are essential. Most students are visual learners.

Others learn by hearing; these are the auditory learners. They prefer to hear new information. They would rather hear a story than read a book. For these students, learning is enhanced by audiotapes and videos. They may be particularly responsive to music.

Some students like to touch objects and manipulate them. These tactile-kinesthetic learners benefit from drawing, creating models, and acting out situations. Of course, a multisensory approach in the classroom will benefit all students.

Global/Analytic Style. This learning style refers to how people process information. The global learner uses the right hemisphere of the brain to focus on spatial and relational processing. This student goes from whole to parts, looking for patterns and determining relationships. The analytic learner uses the left hemisphere of the brain for linear processing. This student moves from the parts to the whole, looking for details on which to base an understanding. While students use both approaches, some tend to rely primarily on one style or the other. Teachers need to model both ways and provide student opportunities to practice both approaches. Many teachers are aware of the two different styles or which one they use most often.

Field-Independent/Field-Dependent. Students who are field-independent like to work alone. They enjoy competition and like individual recognition. Field-dependent students prefer to work with others. They like to collaborate and look to the teacher for direction. Again, teachers need to offer activities related to both styles—providing times when students can work individually without the teacher as well as times when they work with others under the teacher's supervision.

Impulsive/Reflective. Some students are quick to answer questions, make predictions, and guess solutions. These are the impulsive responders. Others are more reflective and take their time to reply. These students do not want to make mistakes and answer carefully to avoid errors. Teachers must provide ample wait time for students to formulate their responses and encourage other students to be patient. Reflectivity is a common mode of response in many cultures.

As you will see in Table 3.1, by planning and implementing a variety of strategies, you will be well equipped to address the learning styles of your students.

Table 3.1   Addressing Learning Styles in the Classroom

Learning Style Type	Sample Teaching Strategies
Audio	Give verbal directions; use direct instruction
Visual	Use pictures, graphic organizers, videos
Tactile-Kinesthetic	Handle artifacts, create models, act out ideas
Global	Look for patterns and relationships
Analytic	Present details for analysis
Field-Dependent	Engage students in cooperative activities
Field-Independent	Develop self-directed projects
Impulsive	Ask for predictions
Reflective	Provide time to formulate response

ADDRESS MULTIPLE INTELLIGENCES

Students also differ in their intellectual capabilities. Howard Gardner (1983) identifies eight categories in which students have strengths and weaknesses. The categories include verbal/linguistic, naturalistic, interpersonal, spatial/visual, musical/rhythmic, intrapersonal, bodily/kinesthetic, and logical/mathematical. In planning lessons, you can use these categories for guidance in developing your presentations and planning corresponding student activities. Again, you want to capitalize upon each student's strength and build weaker areas to ensure that each student is exposed to all categories throughout the year.

An easy way for a beginning teacher to address the multiple intelligences in the classroom is to assign students to complete a project in the "spirit" of a given intelligence or have them choose their own. They can work individually, with a partner, or in a small group. While it is not possible to plan for students to engage in all eight

Table 3.2   Addressing Multiple Intelligences in the Classroom

Intelligence	Teacher Support Suggestions
Verbal/Linguistic (ability to form thoughts and use language for expression)	Provide supplementary reading Hold discussion groups Have students organize and make presentations
Naturalistic (ability to understand the natural world, flora and fauna, and negotiate in the environment)	Have students interact with plants and animals Explore the natural environment
Interpersonal (ability to communicate with others)	Have students work with a partner Involve students in cooperative learning
Spatial/Visual (ability to judge space in relation to people and/or objects)	Bring in artifacts and pictures Organize and present demonstrations Have students create models and pictures
Musical/Rhythmic (ability to create patterns of sound)	Play different types of music Use jingles, chants, and songs as a way of introducing and retaining information Have students put on musical presentations
Intrapersonal (ability to think about thinking, reflect, and self-assess)	Provide students with time to reflect and self-assess Have students create journals
Bodily/Kinesthetic (ability to move skillfully and manipulate objects)	Have students create and perform skits, role-plays, and simulations
Logical/Mathematical (ability to discern logical or numerical patterns)	Have students categorize information, find sequences and cause-and-effect relationships Utilize inquiry methods and project-based learning

categories for each lesson, it is possible for you to give students the opportunity to explore each during the course of the year.

You will find you can address students' learning styles and multiple intelligences at the same time. Through discussion, writing, and various demonstrations of performance, you will become more and more familiar with each student's personality and individual needs and interests.

INVESTIGATE STUDENTS' NEEDS AND SPECIAL SERVICES

In today's schools, students with special needs are placed in the least restrictive environment possible (Karten, 2004). Therefore you are likely to have students with varying abilities in your classroom. You may have students who are blind or have visual impairments, students who are deaf or have hearing impairments, along with students who have speech or language impairments, other physical impairments, learning disabilities, attention deficit disorders, mental retardation, or emotional disturbances. Even within each disability category, there will be a wide range of severity of the disability.

It is important to look at the specific profile and IEP of each student to learn individual strengths and weaknesses. The special education teachers in your school will have suggestions for specific strategies to use with each diagnosed student. Contact the special education facilitator with any questions you might have. You may have an aide or a paraprofessional to help you daily in the classroom.

Other special services may be provided to your students. Some will receive free or reduced price lunches, require individualized medical attention, ride special buses due to physical or emotional needs, and so forth. Your principal, counselor, and grade level team of teachers will keep you informed of various situations that will require your knowledge and assistance.

IDENTIFY GIFTED AND TALENTED STUDENTS

Students with extraordinary intelligences and abilities will also be in your class. These children learn quickly and can absorb more material at higher thinking levels (Tomlinson, 2004). Often, teachers will pretest students to find their prior knowledge or skills and then allow gifted and talented students who show mastery to proceed at an accelerated rate or engage in alternative enrichment activities. Teachers can help these students by providing additional resources and allowing them to work on self-directed projects independently or with partners. Be sure to acknowledge students' progress. Using flexible grouping will enable advanced students to work together to produce projects or presentations reflective of their abilities.

We strongly encourage you to identify one extension for every unit of learning you develop. Extensions need to involve critical thinking and problem solving, and they should include research in the library, on the Internet, and with technology, as in data processing, word processing, and presentation options. Try integrating content across the curriculum including fine and performing arts. Focus on taking gifted and talented students to higher levels of comprehension and application rather than just giving them more of the same and busy work.

All of your students will benefit from exercises that help them to expand their thinking skills. Asking students to explain their answers, explore unknown situations, and imagine alternative creative outcomes will both challenge and delight them. There are unlimited suggestions in teachers' manuals, supplementary materials, and on the Internet.

LEARN MORE AS THE YEAR PROGRESSES

There is much to learn about your students, and they will reveal themselves in many different ways—through their participation in class discussions, their writing, their conversations with you, and their interactions with others that you observe during class and on the playground. You will have opportunities to learn about their families and their community. You will get to know some students more easily than others, so you will need to be patient and give yourself time.

Reflections from a new teacher . . .

A former elementary school student told me years later that the best part of being in third grade was my attending her piano recital. At the beginning of each school year, I gave students a card entitling them to invite me to one out-of-school event. The student had to check the arrangement with his or her parents, the sponsor(s) of the event, and my calendar. I told the students to not presume that I could attend every event especially with little notice. Going to sport events, recitals, parties, and a range of cultural events helped build strong (and lifelong) relationships with all the students and their families that I never anticipated.

As we will explore in greater detail in later chapters, the single most important thing you will do in your work is develop positive, constructive, supportive relationships with your students. These form the foundation for everything else you do to promote learning and growth. The process begins with taking the first steps to learn your students' names and basic interests as soon as you possibly can.

The secret we have explored is to learn to listen carefully. Let your students speak for themselves, restate the students' explanations to check their messages, and encourage students to participate in the decision making and problem solving. These steps take time, yet they will reap huge benefits. Students will see you as a trusted friend who is there to guide and support them. They will see the classroom as *their* classroom, a shared space for teaching and learning. Students will take ownership in their learning and responsibility for their actions. They will grow in their care of themselves, one another, and the world around them.

Construct a School Supply List

As you look ahead to the first day of school, it is time to finalize the student school supply request list. Depending on budget allocations, some schools are able to provide basic supplies, such as paper and pencils and scissors; others are not. You, and perhaps your grade level colleagues, may decide to construct a list of school supplies for your students to bring at the beginning of the school year. Or, the list may be mailed to students or posted in area stores prior to the beginning of the school year, so families can acquire or purchase the requested items in advance of the first day of school.

Try to be reasonable about your lists. Keep in mind that school supplies are costly, especially for families with many children, and children tend to want all new supplies every year. And you need to be prepared for students to come to class empty handed for the first few days. Here are tips: we suggest you note on a copy of your class list who has and who has not brought school supplies. You may need to send reminder notes to some students' families or find other resources (school and parent organizations) to help your economically disadvantaged students get the basic supplies. Then you will need to find a subtle way to give the items to the students, so they won't be embarrassed by their families' financial hardship.

Elementary school supply lists typically include some of these items:

- personal book bag or backpack
- folders with pockets and no brads (plain)
- folders with pockets and brads (plain)
- no. 2 pencils with erasers
- pencil top erasers
- desk storage box (no larger than 6 ½" × 10" × 3 ½")
- box of crayons (no more than 24)
- box of colored pencils (no more than 24) (for older children)
- white glue stick
- pair of scissors (younger children require blunt-tipped scissors)
- ream of lined, three-hole punched notebook paper
- large box of tissues

You will want to modify this list according to the anticipated activities and projected expectations of your learners. As the year goes on, make a list in your planner of ideas that come to you for next year. Also, you might want to ask families to donate items such as magazines, newspapers, yarn scraps, and other identified project items to your classroom throughout the year.

Prepare to Welcome Your Students

The last task is to organize some materials before the students arrive. Place a copy of the class list next to the classroom door, so students and their parents can find their names quickly on the first day of school. Some of your students may arrive on the bus, and you might be required to meet the buses to help welcome your students on the first day. Make another copy of your class list and attach it to a clipboard with some blank paper to make notes with two pencils attached to strings to take with you to the bus, playground, or out into the hallway.

We suggest that you have strips of colorful paper or poster board ready to use as name cards for student desks. Wait until you have met your students, so they can help you spell their names correctly and tell you if they want to use their first and/or middle names, nicknames, or initials. Students can select the color of paper that they prefer. You can use either manuscript or cursive handwriting as is developmentally appropriate. Again, you might want to adhere a sticker of your class motif onto the nameplate. You can prepare a matching nametag for the students, too, so everyone can start associating names with faces.

Students will arrive on the first day with many things including their backpacks holding school supplies, lunches, and perhaps jackets or raingear. For students who bring lunches, we suggest you have a heavy cardboard box or plastic crate ready for storage. In many schools, the storage crates are left in a particular location during lunch so students can leave their boxes and sacks until recess is over.

Students need places to hang backpacks and jackets. Some teachers write the students' names on colorful paper or masking tape and assign a particular hook to each student. This approach can alleviate confusion and help the teacher get possessions back to students easily at the end of the day. You may want to delay identifying hooks until you know what names to use. Students can select any open coat hook on the first day.

Finally, write your name and a short note of welcome on the door! Reflections from a teacher . . .

> Every year I write the same message on my board. It reads, "I am so very glad you are here, and I look forward to a terrific year. Together you and I will learn much about the world and each other. Now look into your desk and get ready to have a great time!" Prior to their arrival, I will have placed a school pencil in each student's desk—sharpened and capped with an extra eraser top. This way, students receive a small welcoming gift from me and are prepared to write on papers when class begins.

GET READY TO HAVE FUN . . .

By the beginning of the first day, you may feel exhausted—and you haven't even started teaching. You have met many responsibilities ranging from establishing safety to creating a comfortable environment and learning about your students and your school. We know you can and will be successful; most of all, we want you to experience both satisfaction and fun. You have been anticipating this first day of your first year for a long time. We are here to help you do well and to enjoy yourself.

Suggested Activities

1. Identify the cultures of your students with which you are least familiar; learn more about them.

2. Make a list of the different activities you might do to learn more about your students.

3. Share examples of how teachers address the multiple intelligences and learning styles of their students in different subjects.

4. Identify resources in your school for gathering information about your students.

CHAPTER FOUR

Beginning and Ending School on the First Day

The first day of school is here. You've practiced your welcoming smile over and over. You are sporting your single best outfit, the one that positively glows with confidence. You feel that you have thought about everything. The bulletin boards are bright and waiting to display student work. The shelves are organized for storing supplies. Materials are fresh and ready to be used for the first lesson. You've written your name and a welcoming message on the board. Now it is time to greet your students and their parents.

MEET YOUR STUDENTS AS THEY ARRIVE

In most elementary schools, young students arrive on the first day with their parents; older returning students may arrive on their own. Parents often come into the school. They want to be sure that their children have found the correct classrooms and that they have arrived safely with their supplies. Parents also are eager to have a little peek at you, as you are new to their school.

Some parents will take a few minutes on the first day of school to say hello and welcome you to the neighborhood. They realize that you will be spending an enormous amount of time with their children and that you play an extremely important role in the academic and social development of their children. Shake parents' hands, listen carefully, nod, and smile. Some parents may share vital information with you, such as that their child needs to buy lunch or is not riding the bus today. Having the class list attached to a clipboard handy will help you record information correctly and immediately. Here's a helpful suggestion: you also may want to post important lunch or travel information on a small clip attached to the classroom door, so you'll remember it when you are leaving the classroom to go to lunch or at the end of the day.

Some parents of younger primary age students may want to stick around for a while. We suggest that you very politely yet diplomatically ask all of the parents to leave within the first half hour of the start of the first day of school. You need to gain your students' total attention and not place your students in the awkward position of trying to listen to the new teacher and keep track of their parents at the same time. In some kindergarten and first grade areas, principals and counselors help escort the parents to the opposite end of the school building in a supportive effort sometimes called "Cookies and Kleenex."

Teachers may greet their new students on the first day by standing next to their classroom doors. Some rooms have doors that open to the outside and to a hallway. Find out the procedure from the other teachers and be ready an hour before school starts. Students and their parents often arrive early on the first day of school.

In some schools, teachers are expected to greet their students outside at assigned locations where the students will line up every morning to enter the school by classrooms. Again, this is where the clipboard with your class list will help you.

TAKE YOUR STUDENTS TO THEIR NEW CLASSROOM

If you meet your students outdoors, you are responsible for helping your students get settled before they go to their classrooms. In some schools, there may be a schoolwide greeting or ceremony that includes reciting the Pledge of Allegiance, singing a patriotic or school song, and listening to announcements. In other schools, these types of openings occur within individual classrooms or over the intercom.

If you meet your students outdoors, be aware of the procedures for entering and moving through the building. You are establishing the patterns and expectations that children need to know and follow daily. You decide who leads the line, how students line up, who holds the door(s), and so forth. However, on the first day of school, you should lead the line and ask a student to hold the door. Later, you can discuss expectations and select helpers in a classroom community meeting.

HELP YOUR STUDENTS MOVE IN

Coming into the room, the students will be checking you out, sizing you up, and making their predictions about whether you are boring or fun, mean or nice. As students enter your classroom, you should give explicit instructions. You probably will need to stand at the door near the coat racks and storage areas to help them unload and get oriented. Remember: they will be arriving with supplies, and they are anxious. They want to know where to sit and who will be sitting next to them. We suggest that you tell them to select any desk and take everything that they brought with them. You can and certainly should assign seats later on or decide a seating arrangement as a community. When students are seated, you can collect group items such as reams of paper and boxes of tissues, place cold lunches in storage crates, and hang backpacks and jackets on coat hooks.

These activities will probably take longer than you predict on the first day, and students may require individual assistance. So here's a valuable secret. Before you go outside to meet the students, place an independent activity sheet or blank paper with either a pencil or some crayons on tables or desks. As you are helping some students to move in, other students can begin to draw a design that you will place on their individual bulletin board clips later in the day or week.

USE NAMETAGS TO LEARN NAMES

You might want to prepare nametags on cutouts to match your classroom theme, such as Mr. Parks' stars, or on self-adhesive papers. If you cut them out of paper, you can ask the students to attach them to their collars with large colorful plastic coated paperclips rather than using straight pins or safety pins. Write only first names in large print or cursive, whatever is appropriate for your students. The nametags are for you and your students.

Have some spare nametags and a pen handy. You might misspell a name or simply get it wrong. You want all of the nametags to look alike so each student feels like an equally valued member of the class. And wear a nametag yourself! This allows you to model exactly what you expect of your students. As you look at their nametags, they can look at yours. You probably will write your title and last name on your nametag. Some veteran teachers are comfortable inserting their first names. We suggest you follow the pattern set by your colleagues in this particular neighborhood.

Then, use each student's name throughout the day. You might want to play a game to help students get to know one another's names quickly. (Ideas for introductory activities are given below.)

Show Students Around the Classroom and School

Your students are eager about everything . . . just like you. They want to know where things are located . . . especially drinking fountains and restrooms. Tell the students where drinking fountains and restrooms are located and how they are expected to act related to each item.

We suggest that, on the first day of school, you take everyone to the drinking fountains and the restrooms in a whole group if these facilities are outside the classroom. Let the students see where both are located, and practice your expectations with your direct supervision. We urge you not only to establish but also to practice and positively reinforce routines frequently throughout the first week of school.

Students will want to know where everything else is located around the classroom and school too. Walk around your classroom slowly, show them where things are located, describe the uses of the various areas, and model your expectations positively. In particular, explain the use of the pencil sharpener, wastebaskets, tissue boxes, and other items that students are expected to use independently and frequently. Emphasize which items or areas students can access on their own, such as bookshelves and supply baskets, as well as which items and areas students should either ask permission to access, such as staplers and scissors, or leave alone, such as your desk drawers.

Each time you take your class to specials or to the cafeteria, you can include a side trip to show them another feature of the school, such as the health office or the library/media center. At that time, model your expectations for clearing off desks and lining up to leave the classroom. The school probably has established procedures for moving through the halls, such as walking in lines, not talking, and keeping hands to oneself. Many of your students will be more famil- iar with the school than you are, yet you want to show your students around as a group so all are acquainted with their surroundings and the expectations associated with each location. You will want to lead your students around the school for the first few days. Then you can step to the end of the line and let one of your students lead. You are likely to be taller than your students, and, from the end of the line, you can see over their heads to monitor their actions while moving between locations. If you are at the front of the line, you cannot monitor actions behind you (Manning & Bucher, 2003).

At the end of the second week of school, you might want to orga- nize a treasure hunt with clues scattered throughout the school. This is a fun activity to develop with the other teachers on your grade level team. Place clues while students are out of the classroom. To find the treasure, students have to know the school and the personnel. This is a wonderful way for everyone to feel more comfortable and to gain a sense of place. It's even more fun when the treasure is a popsicle or watermelon party held outside when the weather is warm!

MAKE INTRODUCTIONS

After you have introduced your students to the basic creature com- forts, you want to introduce yourself to your students and have them introduce themselves to one another and to you. Here is where you begin a wonderful journey, showing confidence and poise. Smile warmly and say, "Now that you know your way around our class- room, let's get to know one another. This is going to be a great school year as we learn more about ourselves and share as a group."

Make sure you have your students' attention when you speak. Project your voice so everyone can hear you. State your name clearly, so students will be able to pronounce it correctly, and have them practice. You are welcome to tell your students your first name, the names of your family members, and more about the important people in your life, if you want. Or you can save this information for another day. Give your students a little background on who you are, but rather than reciting your credentials, tell them a brief story about how you ended up where you are. You are promoting yourself in order to reduce your own anxiety level and help your students feel comfortable with you.

Insights from a new teacher . . .

> I introduce myself using a technique I learned from my mentor teacher. I write the numbers 1–12 on little slips of paper and place the slips in a basket (with at least one number for every two students in the classroom). Working with partners, the students draw numbers from the basket and write a question. The numbers indicate the order questions will be asked. Usually, they want to know if I am married, if I have children, my favorite color, my favorite foods, and what I like to do in my free time. This format sets a wonderful tone for creating a community of learners.

Briefly describe your vision of the class—what the content will be and how the time in class will be spent. Be enthusiastic! Let them know you remember what it was like to be a student, that you know it is important for things to be fun and exciting, and that you intend to accommodate them as best you can. Let your optimism shine!

Move to specifics. Tell them about some of the various activities they will engage in. If you have samples of the types of projects they might do, you could show the samples at this time. Let your students see examples of the textbooks, manipulatives, and other resources they will use. Explain your role as a teacher, and share your expectations of them as students.

Also, be prepared to be tested by someone early in your introduction, some student who is looking for attention, who can't sit still, or perhaps someone who is just being playful. Don't overreact. Just remain calm, poised, and firm. Show that you have a sense of humor, but don't tolerate disrespect. Carefully redirect the student's attention and positively reinforce everyone who is displaying the appropriate actions.

This is the perfect time to look together at the activity that you placed on the students' desks. You can give the students some time to talk quietly with the other students seated at their tables and complete their work. Students will appreciate some time to digest all they have learned during the morning.

After a short while, say 20 minutes, you will want to start some type of more formal introductions. Students can be given a list of questions to ask a partner. For older students, you can include more questions and have students write responses; for young students and those with a limited knowledge of English, you can write one or two questions on the board or on the overhead with pictures; ask students to conduct oral interviews and introductions. Here are some sample questions:

- Where were you born?
- What is your favorite activity outside of school?
- What is your favorite school subject?
- What is your favorite food?
- What kind of music do you like?
- What is your favorite television program?
- What did you do over summer vacation?
- If you could meet anyone in history, whom would you choose?
- What do you think is the most difficult job?
- Do you have a nickname you prefer to be called?
- What would you like other people to know about you?
- If you could live anywhere, where would you go?

Another option is to have students participate in a group consensus activity, such as the following. In groups of four to six people, find examples of the following items that *every* person in the group likes:

- food,
- television program,
- song or musical artist,
- movie/video/DVD, and
- personal characteristic in a friend.

Still another variation is to organize a scavenger hunt type of questionnaire that requires students to interact with others in their search for answers. Or you can simply put them in a circle to get them talking. Whatever you do, however, turn the focus on them in such a way that each person gets the chance to speak.

From a first-year teacher . . .

My favorite way is to have all the students stand in a circle. I say my name and demonstrate an action that has the same number of syllables or beats as my name. Since my name is Ms. Juliano, there are four beats. I say my name, and I clap four times. One clap is above my head, one clap is to the left, one clap is to the right, and one clap is to the front. Then everyone in the class repeats my name and action. We move around the circle to the next student. This student says his or her name and demonstrates an action. We repeat the name and action followed by repeating my name and action. We move around the entire circle. Naturally we forget as we go around the circle so each student has to help lead when we reach that place. This is a wonderful game to learn names and be up on our feet.

Another fun way to learn names is to take the students' photographs sometime during the first day and develop or print the photographs right after school. You can post them on a bulletin board before the students arrive the next day. Students will be thrilled to see their pictures and names displayed in the room (Mitchell & Espeland, 1996).

TRY NOT TO DO TOO MUCH TOO SOON

By now you probably have reached the limits of how long your students can remain still without physically moving around. Most students have a great amount of freedom to be very active in the summer. Although they are eager to be back in school with their friends, some of them resent being back, stuck inside when the weather is still so nice, and there are so many things they would rather be doing. They may have much on their minds, thoughts that have little to do with your agenda, such as which boys or girls they might like and where they will sit at lunch. Also, they are just plain tired, not used to getting up so early.

We suggest you try a few of these activities: go outside for a power walk or engage in a large group activity. Power walks are strolls around and through the playground. Students may walk next to a partner and talk, but they must keep walking. You can tell the students to discuss a particular topic or issue with their partner; or let them discuss a topic of their choice. The idea is to get out of the classroom, physically move around, get some fresh air, and clear the mind. The walk should last approximately 15–20 minutes.

A different approach would be to engage in a group activity either outside or inside. Get a light ball, such as a Koosh or Nerf ball, and stand in a circle with the class. You direct students to announce a word or phrase, giving them a prompt such as "Name something red." Then you call a student's name and toss the ball to that student, who calls out a response. That student calls out another student's name and tosses the ball to that student, who calls out another response. Doing this helps students to learn one another's names quickly and to brainstorm words or phrases related to a particular prompt. (Students will generate all kinds of prompts for you to use in the future.) After everyone has had a turn or you have been able to play the game twice, you can return to the classroom refreshed and ready to continue with first-day activities.

Establish Procedures and Expectations

Two significant procedures you want to establish in your classroom are how you are going to get your students' attention and how students are expected to get your attention (Boynton & Boynton, 2005). Let's talk about your signals to the students first. Signals tell students that it is or near time to make a transition, the noise level is too loud, or you need their immediate attention. You might want to use a small bell or a set of soft chimes to indicate that it is time to stop talking or doing other activities and look to the teacher. Some teachers prefer clapping their hands, sounding out a pattern that students either repeat or complete. Show and tell your students what you will be doing and how they should react. Then practice the motions several times throughout the morning and praise your students for their compliance.

Signals for Attention

- Ring a small handbell
- Play a chime
- Raise a flag or banner
- Clap a rhythm (decide if students should echo in response)
- Open a music box for a song to play quietly
- Raise your hand, lowering your fingers as you count backwards, "5, 4, 3, 2 ,1"
- Use a gentle sounding whistle
- Set a timer (e.g., a kitchen timer) on the overhead projector

The second procedure is how you want students to get your attention. For the first week or so, primary students will call you "Teacher" regardless of your name and what you ask your students to call you. They may also tug on your skirt or pants. They may take your hand to get your attention. Please understand that they have developed a multitude of mechanisms at home to get attention from adults.

You may want students to raise their hands and wait to be called on to speak. You have to tell your students directly that this is the expectation; then you need to practice doing this and praise your students for their compliance. The important part is to be firm, fair, and consistent. You cannot call on students with raised hands some of the time and then respond to students who blurt out at other times. Students will not be sure what to do. The braver students will just blurt out if that seems to work, and the shyer students will do nothing. The students who tend to be more obedient will continue to raise their hands, get frustrated when you respond to the ones blurting out, and begin to lose interest in you. Be careful of what you say you expect and how you reinforce behavior.

Procedures and expectations help keep everyone safe and allow the class to run smoothly. Most elementary schools have created school wide procedures and expectations too. These allow all faculty and staff to hold all students equally accountable and to enforce the same types of discipline regardless of the activity and location. Generally, schoolwide policies are printed and displayed around the school, posted in classrooms, and sent home to parents in handbooks and newsletters. They may include a discipline policy, so students and their parents are aware of significant consequences, such as detention and expulsion.

Not just what you say, but how you communicate with your students concerning these procedures and expectations says much about you to your students. Some teachers present a particular list of classroom rules, often acquired from principals or other teachers, that they want their students to follow. Basically, the teachers tell their students the rules and the consequences if rules are not obeyed. Rules should be stated in the positive. You want students to envision an appropriate behavior, rather than call an action to mind and have to tell themselves not to do it.

Or, you can choose to be democratic; you can begin a discussion with the class and have them give their input on rules. As a whole class, students can suggest three to five important rules for classroom behavior to simplify your classroom management. Creating a few specific rules will give you a manageable reference list that can easily be posted for all to see. Frequently, students will generate the same rules that you already have in mind. You can easily reword students' suggestions or ask leading questions, so the final rule fits your needs. These then become "their" rules rather than "your" rules (DeVries & Zan, 2003).

One variation that requires more time is to first ask the students to work cooperatively in small groups to invent their own rules. Although initially their suggestions may be silly and inappropriate ("We don't need any rules!"), you will be amazed at how wisely they will create exactly the guidelines that are needed. Your job is to draw out of them their own commitment to follow the rules they develop for themselves. This allows you, at a later time, to be able to say to them, "You are the ones who decided that everyone should be respected in this room. I'm just following through on your ideas."

Think of rule setting as constructive discipline and effective class-room management. You are setting up a behavior code that will avoid conflict in the future and provide the students with an environment in which they will be ready to learn and be successful. Here are some of the rules that you might consider implementing, but remember to remain consistent with your school's policies when setting class rules.

Class Rules

- Students should respect space by keeping their hands and feet to themselves.
- Students should respect conversations by raising their hands to talk and by listening carefully when others are talking.
- Students should respect other students by using courteous and considerate language and manners.
- Students should respect all teachers by being ready to learn at their desks with books and materials when class begins.
- Students should respect themselves by doing their best at all times and by having work finished on time and doing all work to the best of their abilities.

Organize Classroom Helpers

Elementary school classrooms are little societies or communities of learners working cooperatively. You do not have the time or energy to take care of everything, and why should you? You have a roomful of people who need and want to become more involved and responsible. Making a helper chart allows everyone to participate and share the load. Table 4.1 is a list of possible tasks with brief descriptions.

Table 4.1   Sample Class Helpers

Class Helper	Responsibilities
Flag Bearer	holds the flag during the morning Pledge of Allegiance
Attendance/Lunch Counter	sees that everyone has checked in and marked a form of lunch
Substitute	collects papers for anyone who is absent
Errand Runner	takes notes to the office or other teachers; goes to office to collect materials
Paper Monitor	distributes papers in class
Assistant	helps in any way necessary
Line Leader	stands at the start of the line
Lunch Crate Keeper	carries the lunch crate to the lunchroom and brings it back to the classroom after lunch recess
Board Eraser	cleans the board at the end of the day
Gardener	waters plants or feeds pets
Room Inspector	checks that the room is in order as expected at the end of the day, i.e., sees that chairs are stacked, trash is picked up, windows are closed, and pencil sharpener is emptied
Coat Monitor	sees that all clothing is claimed in the coat area, including especially lunch boxes and book bags
Mail Monitor	sees that all papers are taken from student mailboxes at the end of the day and may distribute papers to mailboxes too

We suggest that you look around your classroom and identify enough tasks for about half the students. That means if you have 26 students, identify 13 tasks.

Then create a chart with two students assigned to each task; one student serves as the primary helper for one week, and the other student can fill in when the first student is absent or unable to complete the task while also preparing to be the primary helper for the subsequent week. You can make helper charts from library card pockets and index cards, posters with plastic or wooden clothespins, pockets with tongue depressors, and so forth. Place your helper chart near the door and/or your desk, so you, the students, and a substitute teacher can reference it quickly and easily.

INTRODUCE THE DAILY SCHEDULE

On the first day of school, present the daily schedule. Most elementary school teachers start their days following the opening ceremony (as a whole school, grade level, or individual class) with a morning meeting. This is a time to greet one another, take attendance and lunch count, discuss current events (including weather and sports), make announcements, collect notes and papers, and preview the daily schedule and assignments. After the first day, many teachers will ask their older students to write their assignments on a daily record sheet that is kept in a homework folder. Teachers quickly engender a sense of family as students share news and views.

A typical daily schedule with 300 minutes of contact between classroom teacher and students and 30 uninterrupted minutes for lunch) might look like the "Sample Daily Schedule" provided below. In some schools, teachers must follow mandated programs of instruction, some of which regulate the time of instruction and the amount of time on task. In other schools, teachers are responsible for selecting materials and facilitating instruction. Teachers may integrate language arts with science or social studies, plan long-range units of instruction, or team teach with other teachers to maximize resources (Price & Nelson, 2003).

On the first day of school, most students want to see a typical daily schedule, see the accompanying books and materials, and hear about upcoming projects. They have looked forward to being in this particular grade level and are eager about learning what is typically learned. You get to uncork that excitement on the first day!

Sample Daily Schedule

8:30	arrive at school; stay on playground in assigned areas
8:50–9:10	opening/morning meeting
9:10–10:40	language arts (90 minutes)—includes reading, writing, grammar, spelling
10:40–10:55	recess (teachers take turns having recess duty)
10:55–11:55	math (60 minutes)
11:55	prepare for lunch
12:00–12:40	lunch and recess (no recess duty)
12:40–1:00	read aloud/group time
1:00–1:45	science (45 minutes)
1:45–2:15	specials (music and physical education twice per week for four weeks)
2:15–2:45	specials (media and computers twice per week for four weeks)
1:45–2:45	art (daily, for one week every five weeks)
2:45–3:30	social studies (45 minutes)
3:30	close/prep to go home
3:45	dismiss

GIVE STUDENTS A MEANINGFUL ACTIVITY

Teach one of those anticipated lessons on the first day of school (Marzano, Pickering, & Pollack, 2001). When your students go home that afternoon and answer the age-old question of "So . . . what did you learn today?" they will have an energetic response, such as, "I watched how to write my name in cursive!!" Remember how important first impressions can be. You want them to have a taste of something new on the very first day of school!

So make your first lesson engaging. Teach something new that presumes the students have little prior knowledge of the subject. (This makes sure everyone is on equal footing.) Or, pose a stimulating question related to your subject. You want students to leave with something they didn't have when they walked in the door—an innovative idea, a new skill, a fresh interest, a novel piece of information, an "itch that needs scratching."

Memories from an experienced teacher . . .

My favorite start of the year activity was to get large sheets of butcher paper in various colors. Then I would ask students to lie down on a sheet of paper (in the color of their choice), and I would trace their outlines. The students would cut out their own shapes, go through old magazines, and find pictures of items that illustrated their interests. They would cut out and glue the items on their shapes creating body collages. Though this made a fantastic mess, it allowed students to talk freely with one another. We would work on these in preparation for Open House.

Then, at Open House, I would place the body collages in the students' desks and place some of their favorite schoolwork in front of their bodies. The parents just loved this. The students eagerly brought their families to our classroom to show off their creations. (And yes, I would get an incredibly high percentage of parents in attendance!)

PREPARE A FIRST-DAY LETTER TO PARENTS

Here's one of the best suggestions in this book. Write a letter to send home on the first day of school. This should be a one-page letter, hand written or typed, telling families how pleased you are to be their child's teacher and some of the exciting things that you and the students are going to be doing together. You can include one or two announcements, but try to keep reminders to a minimum. This is a letter of welcome.

Reflections from a first-year teacher . . .

I hand wrote my first-day letter during the afternoon recess. I included how many students were enrolled the first day with the number of boys and number of girls and our daily schedule. I told them I was a new teacher and where I went to college. I closed by telling them how I was excited to be a part of their school and that I looked forward to meeting them at the upcoming Open House. Then I added the school's phone number and my school e-mail address, inviting contact at any time. I made copies and read the letter aloud to the students before packing up to go home. I wanted them to know how pleased I was to be their teacher too.

REVIEW THE DAY BEFORE GOING HOME

Don't let the bell end your class; *you* end it by timing your final words to be spoken before the bell rings. As the day is closing, ask your students to take out or distribute a folder to designate for homework and letters or notices to take home. Now is the time to review the events of the day and any assignments. Use the agenda on the board to refresh everyone's memory of the sequence of events, as well as the highlights and accomplishments. Students, especially the younger ones, may not remember what happened six hours earlier in the day, and you want every child to answer the question "How was school today?" well informed and enthusiastic. Say goodbye with a smile.

LOOK FORWARD TO THE NEXT DAY . . .

Yes, it was only Day One. You will be amazed how quickly the time flew and what wonderful children entered your life today. You will be tired and hungry. Stay and work in your classroom for no more than an hour. Then go home, call a good friend, tell them how fantastic you were, how exciting the students were, and dream about Day Two. You get to do it all again; only this time you'll know what you're doing!!

Suggested Activities

1. Interview veteran teachers to find out how they structure the first day of school. What are their greatest challenges, and how do they address them?

2. Draft a letter that you might send home to parents the first day of school.

3. Create a list of classroom helpers that you think you would find helpful. Compare your list with a colleague's list.

4. Begin a portfolio of introduction games and activities.

CHAPTER FIVE

Developing Meaningful Curriculum

Talking about "the curriculum" probably brings to mind a special notebook commonly known as a scope and sequence guide that contains essential documents and lists of classroom expectations for each grade level and subject area. As you look around, you will typically find this notebook on a dusty shelf in a teacher's cabinet or the school's professional library. We have found that, while most teachers acknowledge that the scope and sequence guide exists, they use it infrequently as time goes on. However, you'll find it a helpful resource.

> "You have to teach a lot of good stuff, like math."
>
> —Vanessa, age 7, Grade 1

However, curriculum is much more than a notebook of district documents and classroom expectations. Curriculum is the word used to describe *everything* that happens around schools and in classrooms—everything before, during, and after school hours that involves the students, teachers, and learning community (Oliva, 2004). An important secret for teachers to understand early in their careers is that the curriculum identifies the content, processes, and context of the *entire* educational environment. It involves the mission, beliefs, and all the extraordinary features of the school; for example, perhaps it is a special type of school, such as a magnet school or one with a distinct theme or emphasis.

UNDERSTAND KEY CONCEPTS

Curriculum *content* attends to *what* is to be taught and learned; curriculum *processes* entail *how* content is to be taught and learned. Curriculum *context* describes several different vital aspects related to the classroom including the environment—*where, when,* and *how* teaching and learning will occur—and the *culture*—*who* the teachers are, *who* the learners are, and *who* makes up both the local and global communities (along with the range of characteristics typical of each group). Curriculum *context* also depicts purposes—*why* this particular teaching and learning will occur and *how* it fits with the classroom and/or school. Crucial to overall curricular success, the context includes application and assessment—*how* teaching and learning are planned, facilitated, monitored, measured, and reported. Content, processes, and context have both presence and power in every teaching/learning event. It is imperative for you to be aware of these terms and to apply the concepts mindfully as you continually develop, facilitate, and evaluate curriculum throughout the school year. Table 5.1 reviews the terms and their corresponding questions.

Table 5.1   Curriculum Terms and Corresponding Questions

Curriculum Term	*Question To Be Answered*
CONTENT	What is to be taught and learned?
PROCESS	How is the content to be taught and learned?
CONTEXT	When, where, how, and why will the teaching, learning, and assessment occur?
CULTURE	Who are the teacher(s) and students? Who are the members of the community?

CLARIFY GOALS AND OBJECTIVES

In most elementary school classrooms, curriculum content consists of all the subject areas and is usually based on state academic content standards. These include literacy (or the language arts including reading, writing, spelling, speaking, listening, and second languages), math, science, social studies (including economics, geography, government/citizenship, history), art, music, physical education, health, media, and technology. For each content or subject area, the curriculum frames the desired knowledge in broad general outcomes guiding all PreK–12 classrooms holistically. These outcomes are called *content goals* and help establish overarching purposes for learning (Airasian, 2000).

An example of a PreK–12 curriculum content goal for social studies might state, "Students will acquire a foundation of knowledge related to the major elements of geographical study, analysis, and their relationships to changes in society and environment."

For each particular content or subject area goal, the curriculum is subdivided into grade level *objectives*. Objectives stipulate the precise outcomes or competencies that are considered developmentally appropriate for an average student in a particular grade level; students must understand and demonstrate these competencies at a predetermined level of proficiency.

An example of a curriculum content objective for second grade social studies might state, "Students will compare how land is used in urban, suburban, and rural environments."

The curriculum content goals and objectives guide you because they say what is to be taught and learned as the foundation of all your classroom lesson plans and learning experiences.

Both content goals and content objectives involve processes or skills. Similar to content goals, some of the curriculum processes are broad general outcomes called *process goals*.

An example of a curriculum process goal might state, "Students will demonstrate the ability to gather, analyze, and apply information and ideas."

This process goal is relevant to all content areas and all grade levels. Again, the more specific processing outcome is called a curriculum *process objective*.

An example of a curriculum process objective for second grade social studies might state, "Students will construct maps with titles, keys, and legends."

Second graders not only learn new knowledge, they also learn new skills to demonstrate fulfillment of the content and process expectations.

Curriculum context is the third broad general concept, yet it is an equally important term that incorporates everything to ensure successful development, facilitation, and evaluation of the content and process. As previously explained, curriculum context involves *when* and *where* or the time and space that teaching and learning will occur. Context describes whether a particular classroom lesson will occur as an independent learning experience or whether it will be combined with other content area or process objectives as an integrated lesson (Manning, Manning, & Long, 1994).

For example, in order to help second grade students fulfill the process objective of drawing maps with titles, keys, and legends, first you focus on a selected group of students, and then you begin to make a series of decisions. You decide whether this lesson will be taught earlier or later during the school year, and as an independent lesson or part of a larger unit of study, or both. The outcomes can be achieved via a social studies unit aimed at getting to know the school and community or through a literacy unit developed to extend students' understanding of a selected story. You will decide if this learning experience will be an introductory, review, or mastery exercise. And you determine whether maps will be drawn by each student, with partners, in small groups (and with or without parental/ family assistance).

Follow a Curriculum Checklist to Fit Context

Then you select what tools will be necessary and optional for drawing the maps, the criteria required and optional on each map, and the deadline for producing the maps. In addition, you identify how to meet special learning needs; how both the map-making products and processes will be assessed; whether the maps will be shared with other groups of students or families; and, if so, how sharing will occur (and be measured). The checklist below lists sample questions to guide you in the decisions. Contextualizing the content and process compels you to consider the curriculum holistically—to ensure relevance and significance for the learner, and for yourself as a teacher, in relationship to the sequence of learning events. At the end of the chapter, we provide a detailed example.

Curriculum Decision Checklist: Questions in Determining Curriculum

___ When during the year will objectives be covered?

___ Will it be an independent lesson or unit of study?

___ To what degree will literacy skills be integrated?

___ What will the specific learning experiences look like?

___ What materials and tools will be needed?

___ What space arrangements will facilitate the learning?

___ What adaptations and modifications will be made?

___ How will students be grouped?

___ How will learning be measured?

___ If appropriate, how will learning be shared?

___ How much time will be spent on instruction and assessment?

REVIEW NATIONAL STANDARDS AND PURPOSES

The grade level academic expectations for each content or subject area, which are found in the school district scope and sequence guides, are based upon standards and purposes written by various national councils of educators or by professional learned societies specializing in specific content areas. These councils include the National Council of Teachers of English (NCTE), the National Council of Teachers of Mathematics (NCTM), the National Science Teachers Association (NSTA), and the National Council for the Social Studies (NCSS).

Each national council meets annually and is organized around numerous committees consisting of elementary and secondary teachers and principals. Teacher educators and educational researchers also participate; they continually review their works, examine theories, and share practices to inform teachers and strengthen education in their different content fields of study. For example, the second-grade level social studies objective stating "Students will construct maps with titles, keys, and legends" is based upon NCSS Theme III: "People, Places, and Environments" and fulfills the purposes of "social understanding" (applying knowledge and skills from a social science) and "self-sufficiency" (taking care of one's self) (Gallavan, in press). All content or subject areas have identified standards and purposes that can be taught independently or combined with those from other content or subject areas to create integrated learning experiences.

It is important for you to understand, apply, and appreciate the national standards and purposes as viable connections to your individual personal, professional, and pedagogical experiences. You should be able to find concrete examples of each standard in your daily lives (the personal connection), as part of your becoming an educator (the professional connection), and as a part of your escalating teaching repertoire (the pedagogical connection). For example, the National Council of Teachers of English has established 12 standards. Standard 5 states, "Students employ a wide range of strategies as they write and use different writing process elements appropriately to communicate with different audiences for a variety of purposes."

To exemplify her three connections to this standard, one teacher brought a dinner menu from her favorite restaurant (the personal connection). The text on a restaurant menu tends to follow a format unique to menus that is fundamental for educated citizens to be able to read, understand, and use (the professional connection). This teacher incorporated a menu reading/writing assignment into one of her literacy lessons to expose her students to this type of text, to enrich her students' literacy levels, and to advance their multicultural awareness (the pedagogical connections). These connections fortify your knowledge, application, and appreciation of the national standards and purposes for each of the professional learned societies and enhance your future classroom success.

ACCESS STATE ACADEMIC EXPECTATIONS

Each state has crafted academic expectations that establish the grade level outcomes as goals and objectives. While education is a responsibility primarily of state governments, it is evident that students and teachers move frequently within states and from state to state. Some consistencies must exist to ensure that students starting a particular grade level in one state can continue and complete the grade level successfully in another state. For example, most states follow the same expanding horizons approach in social studies education. Starting with the concept of self in kindergarten, the curriculum content and processes move outward as if following the ripple created by a pebble dropped in water. Third graders study cities, fourth graders study states; fifth graders study the United States; sixth graders study the world.

LEARN SCHOOL DISTRICT SCOPE AND SEQUENCE

This chapter began by describing the notebook known as a scope and sequence guide. It includes the scope—a finite span of academic expectations set for a particular grade level—balanced with the sequence—the order that academic expectations should be introduced, reviewed, and mastered in each grade level. For some teachers, especially new teachers, the school district scope and sequence guide often becomes one of the more useful documents you will reference throughout your teaching career. You will want to get a copy of the standards for your grade level and content areas from the scope and sequence guide or the state and district Web sites.

When developing their individual PreK–12 curriculum, most local school districts have drawn from both the national standards and purposes as well as from their own state's grade level curriculum and expectations in each content area. School district personnel may have selected explicit approaches to frame the teaching and learning in their schools and classrooms, and these are highlighted in their scope and sequence guides. For example, some school districts highly value team teaching in the primary grades, cross grade level grouping in the intermediate grades, interdisciplinary academies or houses in the middle school grades, and block scheduling in the high school grades. Some school districts feature specific academic programs in reading, spelling, math, and technology. Other school districts focus on processes such as critical thinking, project learning, and service learning. And some school districts emphasize community-building projects such as student leadership, afterschool activities, and life-long learning opportunities. All of these are described in scope and sequence guides as integral parts of the curriculum.

In many districts, additional information is included in the scope and sequence binder or on Web sites. Suggestions for setting up classroom environments, emergency procedures, learning centers, daily schedules, classroom management plans, and classroom discipline plans also may be found there. Many school districts distribute detailed long-range curriculum development and planning strategies, instructional strategies, assessment strategies, parent conference ideas, and substitute teacher plans. A yearly handbook or updated information sheets communicate current school calendars, important contact information, report forms, faculty development inservices, and workshop information. If your district does not provide these types of information, we strongly encourage you to become familiar with the state academic expectations and to use the scope and sequence information produced by some of the larger school districts in your state. Check your state department of education's Web site to identify the higher achieving schools and school districts.

CONSIDER YOUR SCHOOL'S MISSION

Most schools have crafted mission and belief statements. In general, mission and belief statements are written in overarching phrases to unite and guide everyone within a defined geographic learning community. Mission statements tend to set long-range purposes that are more global and all encompassing. For example, here are some schools' mission statements:

- "We focus on challenging students to achieve their creative and physical potential in order to become active members of a responsible, contributing citizenry."
- "Our mission is to put first the inquisitive children of today in support of fulfilling their quest in becoming active adults of tomorrow."

Belief statements tend to determine more immediate and concrete operating principles related to students, teachers, and the community; these statements guide content, pedagogy, and curriculum. Here is example of one school's belief statement:

> All children can learn and achieve; each child is a unique individual. Children learn best in caring atmospheres where respect for self and others enhances society. There should be continuity in all academic areas featuring problem solving and critical thinking to prepare learners for life. The school should be safe, clean, and conducive to teaching and learning; students, parents, educators, and community must work together to maximize success.

Reviewing mission and belief statements will give you a sense of shared community and collaboration as well as help you set achievable goals and purposes. The mission and belief statements are integral for understanding what is important to a particular school.

DESIGN A YEARLONG PLAN

Let's review. You understand the key concepts of curriculum, and you are well acquainted with national standards and purposes. You know your state academic standards and grade level expectations or objectives and have accessed, if available, your school district's scope and sequence guides. You are also equipped with the school's mission and belief statements, so you are ready to develop your own classroom's curriculum. Here is a course of action to help you get started.

First, it is recommended that you examine the entire list of (state and school district) grade level objectives. Ask yourself if one item needs to be learned prior to learning another item. Obviously, these items have to be arranged in a chronological order to accommodate this need. For example, many math programs follow a set pattern. Students may need to learn specific knowledge and skills in one chapter of the textbook before learning new skills in the following chapters. This same thinking may or may not apply to knowledge and skills within literacy, science, and social studies.

Second, it is recommended that you consider whether content will be taught within independent subject areas. Many expectations for literacy, science, and social studies can be taught and learned independently or integrated with one another. Math frequently tends to be taught and learned independently. Yet, math and other content areas may be addressed with an integrated approach to provide context and connections to the students' everyday world.

For example, when studying nutrition for science and writing reports about eating habits for social studies, fourth graders may be reading a novel in language arts that involves food. In this example, math can be included too. Students can calculate the number of calories they eat, their percentage of body fat, and the cost of food (eating at home as well as in various restaurants). Media and technology lend themselves readily to these integrated learning experiences; likewise, the specials teachers, especially physical education teachers, can also relate their lessons. This integrated unit of learning can connect classrooms and families too.

THINK ABOUT CONTENT AND SKILLS

Next, consider different skills or processes applicable to learning the content. Vary the teaching strategies and learning experiences through which students acquire and express new knowledge and skills. In this way, you provide a balance of explorations to fulfill all of Bloom's levels of inquiry and Gardner's multiple intelligences, building upon students' strengths and improving deficit areas. You can design a basic frame to which your students can add their own ideas about learning activities for the entire group. Or you, with your class or independently, may decide to create a menu of options from which students can select individual projects or small group assignments. When students self-select and self-direct their investigations, they move to a higher level of responsibility for their learning. As they share the outcomes of these individual or small-group projects, more students are exposed to additional and different kinds of knowledge and skills. And these are the ultimate goals for all students and classrooms!

When designing long-range curriculum, it is highly recommended that content and processes from all subject areas be combined or integrated as much as possible and focused around central themes. This approach strengthens the learning in that students understand the new concepts from a multitude of perspectives, can express the new learning in a variety of formats, and can apply the new learning authentically within their own lives. The overall learning is more genuine as it replicates how people actually learn about life.

One effective approach in making long-range plans is to create charts that match the school year calendar, e.g., four quarters, trimesters, etc. Within each of these time frames, you can group the grade level objectives for one content area in a logical sequence so that every expectation is assigned to a time frame. One successful teacher liked to begin with social studies. In the first quarter, he would assign the theme of "getting acquainted with self, one another, school, community, and geography." In the second quarter, he would place the theme "exploring cultures, history, economics, and nutrition," aligning this exploration with the diversity of fall and winter holidays. In the third quarter, he would place themes focused on "citizenship, government, and history," aligning these with issues of leadership. In the fourth quarter, he would place themes associated with "community connections" to bring the year's learning together.

From these initial placements, the teacher would add objectives for science, literacy, and, when possible, math. He would extend the integrated units of learning with expectations from media, technology, health, and the specials. He found that most specials teachers were eager to collaborate with his curricular development and could add much more to the students' projects. Once he had constructed this conceptual framework, he could begin to add the rest of the curriculum for each quarter and build upon or scaffold the learning from one quarter to the next (Clay & Cazden, 1992; Vygotsky, 1978).

You can continue planning by noting the dates of school vacations, standardized testing, school events, report cards, and parent conferences. This long-range planning gives you a global view of how you will proceed and points out the necessity of keeping a steady pace throughout the year. Most likely, there will be adjustments to the plan along the way, but your initial outline will give you a good idea of how to function.

ALIGN CURRICULUM WITH INSTRUCTION AND ASSESSMENT

Once you have established a conceptual framework for your curriculum, it's time to identify specific objectives and then design instruction aligned to assessments.

From a new teacher . . .

> I taught map making in the first quarter by dividing the class into cooperative learning groups of three to five students. Each group was given a map of the school and was asked to design a treasure map with six stops for another group to follow. The clue for the next stop could not be opened until the group had located the previous stop. I modeled how to write and follow clues. Other teachers throughout the school were involved in monitoring my students' passage through each stop of their treasure maps. This assignment lasted three days with writing, practicing, and following maps. Students just loved it! And it worked for me too!

This Treasure Map assignment would fulfill several content and process objectives in social studies and literacy while providing the foundation for future map reading and map making throughout the school year. It can be aligned with assessments for writing clues, drawing maps, and working in a group to follow directions. There are many assessment decisions to make in advance of the assignment. For example, will the students be assessed for their map making before other students follow their maps? If so, what criteria would be set prior to the assignment and discussed with the students? How many points or what percentage of the total grade will be given to the map making? Would this part of the grade reflect only the written product, or would part of the grade include working in the cooperative group? If part of the grade is working together, what are the criteria and feedback for assessment? How do you ensure that each member of the cooperative learning group contributes equally to the map making and map following? These are just some of the questions that you must address while designing this assignment. Clearly, it is important to align the curriculum, instruction, and assessment for each assignment, ensuring that each part fits the whole, and each objective fits the goal. We continue this discussion in Chapter 6.

MATCH THE CURRICULUM TO YOUR STUDENTS

All of the procedures for developing curriculum described to this point have been missing the chief element: the students! This chapter was written to prepare you for any situation. Now you must mold your aligned curriculum (including the content, processes, and context), your instruction, and your assessments with your young learners.

Summary List of Factors to Consider in Curriculum Design

___ National Standards and Purposes

___ State Academic Standards

___ District Scope and Sequence

___ District Mission and Belief Statements

___ Integrated or Independent Lessons

___ Sequence

___ Alignment of Content and Processes With Instruction

___ Alignment of Instruction With Assessment

___ Available Materials and Resources

Some of you will be teaching one grade level; others will be teaching combined grade levels. But you know that not every child in a particular grade is functioning at that grade level, and certainly not all children meet grade level expectations in every content or subject area. The challenge for every teacher every year is to match the grade level curriculum with the abilities, needs, and interests of the students in that classroom. You have three main goals: create a community of learners, advance this community's learning as much as possible and in as many different ways as possible, and end the year knowing that you did your best for each child regardless of your accumulated resources and years of experience. You are ready to begin.

"I liked second grade when the teacher let us work together, like with the building blocks to make towers. We can be a little noisy and a little messy."

—Maria, age 9, Grade 3

TAKE TIME TO REFLECT, EVALUATE, AND REVISE . . .

Developing meaningful curriculum will be one of your greatest responsibilities and excitements. You will look forward to starting each school year and designing innovative curriculum.

Notes from a new teacher . . .

I kept a journal throughout my first year of teaching. I would take notes during the day and record them on my computer at night. I tried to think of at least one new discovery and one significant accomplishment each day. Then I would write some questions. Finally, I created a T-chart for each subject area. On the left, I recorded what we did. On the right, I recorded what I would do differently. During the first few weeks of summer vacation, I reviewed my notes and revised plans for the entire next school year. It was amazing to see what I had written, the insights I had along the way, and how I had changed.

As you reflect on each day, evaluate honestly. What worked for your learners? What worked for you? What worked in that time and space? In these ways, you revise the content, the processes, and the context to stay fresh and ready. You might decide to make notes in your planner rather than a journal. As you acquire new materials and resources for your classrooms, you can add to growing units of learning in ways that you could not imagine as a new teacher. Teaching is the one career that you get to start anew every year; developing the curriculum is the means to this end.

Suggested Activities

1. Give examples of how curriculum is dynamic, and discuss how that impacts the classroom teacher.

2. Draft a yearlong plan, taking into consideration the school calendar and required standardized assessments. Compare it with a colleague's plan.

3. Keep records in your notebook throughout the year of what worked and what didn't work to use as a reference in planning for next year.

4. Ask a colleague for one new idea about organizing curriculum for you to try next year.

CHAPTER SIX

Planning Instruction and Assessment

"What are we going to do today?" This is often the question that students ask as they come into the classroom. Your students will be eager to see what is new and to hear about what they are going to do. Elementary school students like to be actively engaged in their own learning as they make new discoveries and connections. You have the best job in the world! You get to design the instructional and assessment activities.

SELECT A LESSON PLAN FORMAT

As the instructional leader in the classroom, you need to be ready. Once the bell rings and the students come into your classroom, their eyes will be on you. This is the moment for you to take charge. A well-developed plan will be your guide. It will provide you with your selected objectives for the day, a sequence of activities, a list of needed resources, and the corresponding assessments (Oosterhof, 2003).

While school districts or building principals may request a particular format, there are common elements found in most lesson plans. Two lesson plan formats are included here for your consideration. Table 6.1 presents a detailed plan, which is similar to what is taught in university methods courses; Table 6.2 is an abbreviated version, which most elementary school classroom teachers follow.

Table 6.1   Detailed Lesson Plan

1. Title of Lesson:	Catchy name that describes the desired knowledge, skills, and dispositions
2. Goal:	General knowledge and skills that students will have at the end of the lesson, unit, and school year. The goals frequently align with national and state standards.
3. Objective:	Specific knowledge and skills that students will demonstrate at the end of the lesson, usually stated as "The learner will . . ." The objectives frequently align with district scope and sequence academic expectations; the objectives can address what students will know, do, understand, believe, or feel.
4. Inquiry Question:	Captivating prompt to help you set the tone and begin the learning; it models an investigative approach that is curious and constructivist.

5. Preparation:	Detailed descriptions of
	a. supplies and materials
	b. time and space
	c. required background knowledge and prior experiences
	d. anticipatory set and motivation
	e. accommodations and modifications for
	   1. English language learners
	   2. gifted and talented students
	   3. special education students
	   4. individual instruction of any kind
	f. connections to life, living, and the community

6. Procedures:	Specific steps for completing this lesson; usually these are stated as "The teacher will . . ." balanced with "The student will. . . ." Be sure to include concrete examples yet have room for individual expression regarding learning and outcomes.
7. Integration:	Authentic ideas for connecting this particular learning experience with language arts, math, science, social studies, health, technology, and fine arts
8. Vocabulary:	Key words to emphasize during this learning experience
9. Guided Practice:	Meaningful activities that students complete in class with the guidance of the teacher, so the teacher can ensure that all students understand expectations
10. Independent Practice:	Practical activities that students complete either independently in class or outside of class to practice and apply the new learning
11. Closure:	Revisiting and recapping the highlights of the learning processes and lesson outcomes with students at end of the lesson
12. Assessment:	Performance-based demonstration that each student has acquired and mastered the objectives
13. Evaluation:	Mindful reflection upon the effectiveness of the overall learning experience, student engagement and outcomes, and teaching

Table 6.2   Quick and Easy Lesson Plan

1. Goals and Objectives	1. The learner will . . .	1. what students will know and be able to do specifically at the end of the lesson
2. Standards and Expectations	2. to fulfill . . .	2. statements of general knowledge and skills
3. Preparations and Procedures	3. using . . .	3. supplies and materials, description of student activities
4. Assessment and Evaluation	4. demonstrated by . . .	4. entry level, progress monitoring, and summative assessment

Now you need to be sure that your students are motivated and can achieve the grade level goals and expectations. You have to develop lesson plans that capture and keep your students' attention, are implemented so that they can participate completely, and include a variety of assessment procedures to not only show you they have learned but also prepare them for required standardized testing (Brophy, 1998).

CONSIDER YOUR STUDENTS' NEEDS

Here are some considerations and suggestions for various groups of students with whom you will be working:

- *English Language Learners.* As these students need to develop literacy in English, it is helpful to look at their levels of language ability and then design activities and assessments accordingly. A brief overview of the five levels of language proficiency, the characteristics of students at each level, and corresponding sample teaching strategies follows in Table 6.3.
- *Special Needs Students.* This population of students will have Individualized Education Plans (IEPs) indicating the modifications and adaptations to be made for those who qualify for services (Smith, Polloway, Patton, & Dowdy, 2006). Many changes can easily be made in the classroom with

Table 6.3   Overview of Language Development Proficiency Levels and Student Characteristics With Corresponding Strategies for Teachers

Level of Proficiency	Student Characteristics	Teaching Strategies
Level 1: Preproduction	Recognizes words Uses nonverbal responses	Use gestures with speech, pictures, models, demonstrations
Level 2: Early Production	Understands main ideas Repeats words heard frequently	Build on student knowledge Ask who, what, where, when questions
Level 3: Beginning Speech	Initiates conversations Mispronounces words Expands vocabulary	Introduce reading and writing Correct speech in context
Level 4: Intermediate Fluency	Uses longer sentences Begins to think in English	Provide opportunity to use language Ask open-ended questions
Level 5: Advanced Fluency	Produces written and oral language	Focus on reading and writing skills

respect to the learning activities and the environments for special needs students. Common changes are listed below. The assessments you use for your special needs students will have to be similarly modified. Read each IEP for guidance.

Considerations for Special Needs Students

- breaking assignments into small chunks
- using graphic organizers
- narrowing the focus to key terms and concepts
- allowing extra time for completion of tasks
- using a computer or other assistive technologies
- having someone else write for them
- having someone read to them
- color coding or otherwise organizing materials

- *Struggling Readers.* Regardless of their language backgrounds, some students will need additional support in reading. Implementing before, during, and after the reading strategies facilitates comprehension and retention. Suggestions are found in Table 6.4.

Table 6.4   Literacy Strategies

Graphic Organizers: Examples include time lines, Venn diagrams, cause and effect charts, and outlines; use them before, during, and after reading.

KWL(H): At the start of the study, have students identify what they **K**now and what they **W**ant to know and then, at the end of the study, what they have **L**earned (and **H**ow they know what they learned).

Pictures, Objects, Models: Use items or pictures to give students a visual reference for what they will be reading about.

SQ3-R: Use the **S**urvey, **Q**uestion, **R**ead, **R**ecite, and **R**eview method with text.

Textbook Scavenger Hunts: Acquaint students with textbook features at the beginning of the year.

Vocabulary Cards: Have students use or create cards with picture references and definitions.

Word Walls: Create a display of related vocabulary on a bulletin board. Include pictures of new words and terms.

You will want to get to know your students quickly so you can plan lessons that appeal to them, capitalize upon their learning styles, provide for their weaknesses, and bolster their confidence. Your students want to be challenged and to be successful. And, most of all, your students want to enjoy school and please you.

Since most of your students stay with you all day for every subject area, you need to make connections among all parts of the curriculum content and balance the instructional practices while building a cohesive community of learners. You have to consider how your lessons will fit together throughout the day and from day to day in terms of your grade level of learners' usual attention span. Think about the types of activities you will be implementing so everyone's energies flow smoothly through the day. You want to balance quiet, independent working activities with noisier interactive, group activities. There should be time for sitting still and time for moving around.

"I like it when we can do our work with our friends and have more breaks, especially water and bathroom breaks. I like to get up and move around."

—Riley, age 9, Grade 3

You might want to select an academic theme for your classroom and lessons to coordinate the curricular content. We suggest you start with your science and social studies expectations; these content areas give you the substance around which you can fit everything else. You can find many different books for reading that offer both fiction and nonfiction options. Try to keep the learning simple and natural, especially during your first year of teaching. Many ideas will bombard you as you start your plans. Record them in your journal or the back of your planner; you have a lifelong career ahead of you to use them.

Analyze Your Teaching Style

Everyone teaches in a unique fashion, and that's great. Just think of all the teachers you had in school. Aren't you glad no two of them were exactly alike? Your preferred teaching style may or may not match the preferred learning styles of your students or the preferred approaches of your grade level colleagues or the school administration. Be aware of your school's philosophy and expectations.

Most schools welcome many different teaching styles and hope that you will use a variety of styles throughout the day and within every content area. You want to incorporate whole group instruction, small group instruction and activities, partner activities, individual instruction, time at learning centers and stations, and time for choice and independent learning. You want to be the teacher, and you want the students to be teachers. You want your students to arrange desks and chairs in rows, groups, circles, and so forth. You want your students to stand, sit on the floor, and walk around, both indoors and outdoors. Be sure to check out suggestions supporting constructivist classrooms (Brooks & Brooks, 1999).

You want to make some decisions; you want your students to make some decisions. You want to practice voting, coming to consensus, and agreeing to compromise. Sometimes you want to call on particular students for particular reasons during a class discussion; sometimes you want the conversation to be more random. You want to acquire a multitude of approaches for calling on students and involving them in the learning process. These changes will captivate your students' attention, especially when you know the new learning might be more difficult or less exciting than usual.

"Another time we dressed up like a character in a book for a book report."

—Jose, age 11, Grade 5

BEGIN WITH OBJECTIVES AND ASSESSMENTS

As you introduce individual lessons, you want to tell the students what they are going to learn, a purpose or reason for learning, and how they are going to demonstrate their learning. Many of you have heard that you need to state the *objective*. Objectives address learning that is cognitive (about content), psychomotor (about skills), or affective (about feelings and attitudes). It is easiest to write objectives using sentences that begin with "The student will . . ." and follow with a verb that indicates performance, such as "define," "identify," "compare," or "solve." You will want to identify something for students to do that you can readily observe, so you can follow their progress. Some principals expect you to write the objectives on the board for students to refer to throughout the lesson and keep everyone grounded. You may find this strategy helpful to remind you to identify the objective(s) for every lesson. It also looks smart when parents, colleagues, and principals drop in to see you. And they will drop in to see you!

Then, think about the kinds of assessments that will tell if and to what degree the students have mastered the objectives. After selecting your objectives, you identify your desired outcomes, which are typically thought of as the last segment in designing a lesson or unit. By working "backwards," you then align the instruction with the anticipated outcomes. This approach has become more popular with recent trends in accountability (Wiggins & McTighe, 2006). Furthermore, students are expected to demonstrate knowledge and skills in a variety of ways, as is seen on state standardized tests. By incorporating in their daily assignments instructional activities that prepare students for these types of tests, you enhance your students' abilities to score well on the tests.

Let's say you want your students to show they know their state capital and five state symbols to fulfill the state standards and school district academic expectations. You decide to assess this knowledge using a 10-question written multiple choice test.

Working backwards, you design the teaching and learning so students can demonstrate successful achievement. You decide to ask students what they think the state capital is and what they know about other state symbols, form investigative groups to look at resources you have made available, and ask for reports in 30 minutes. Then you give each student a sheet showing pictures of each item for them to color and add to their state study folders.

You inform the students that they will be taking a written multiple choice test on a specific upcoming date and that the test will ask them to select the name of the state capital and each of the state symbols from a list. Write a sample assessment item on the board or overhead transparency, so students understand the content and format of the assessment. You can show them all of the questions in advance if you feel it would be helpful for students to be successful. You must decide what is developmentally appropriate for your grade level and your students. Tests should not be a surprise. You did not like it when this occurred in your schooling; do not do this to your students. You do not want to be disappointed when your students do not accomplish the outcomes you give them or start to dislike school needlessly.

"One teacher wouldn't tell us when we would have pop quizzes. I don't mind learning, but I don't want to worry about what the teacher is going to do to us."

—Thuy, age 11, Grade 5

PROVIDE AUTHENTIC AND ALTERNATIVE ASSESSMENTS

Your time and energy are limited, so everything you do must have a reason and contribute to accountability. Assessment reports how well your students have learned and can demonstrate knowledge and skills.

Assessment serves five functions for students to demonstrate (Stiggins, 2004):

1. knowledge and understanding—answers the questions of who, what, and where;

2. logic and reasoning—answers the questions of why, why not, and how do you know;

3. skills and demonstration—answers the questions of how and can you show me;

4. productivity and creativity—answers the questions of what else and how might you . . . ; and

5. outlooks and dispositions—answers the questions of what do you think is important, how do you feel, and how might someone else think or feel.

You can acquire feedback through five different structures:

1. selected responses—written multiple choice, matching, true/false, fill in the blanks, or checklist—all picked from a provided list;

2. constructed essays—written words, sentences, paragraphs, articles, stories, and so forth—all responses originating from the student's memory;

3. demonstrated performances—actions and presentations shown to an individual or to a group either spontaneous or prepared—frequently integrating constructed essays and personal communications;

4. personal communications—answers to questions—oral or verbal responses through formal or informal conversations; and

5. combinations of any of the four structures listed here.

"I like when teachers give us projects to do."

—Angela, age 8, Grade 2

A list of alternative assessments is provided below. Explore with students which types they think are the most fun!

A to Z of Alternative Assessments

Advertisement, artifact replicas, animated stories

Brochure

Collage, children's book

Dance, debate, demonstration, diorama, drawings

Editorial

Fashion show

Games, graphic organizers

Historical portrayal of person or event

Interview

Journal entry

K-W-L-H chart

Letter, learning log

Maps, mobiles, models, movie, museum

Newscast

Obituary

Photographic essay, play, poem, political cartoon, poster

Questionnaire and results analysis, quilt

Role-play

Simulation, slide show, song, speech, storyboard

Television program, think-aloud

Unit summary with illustrations

Video documentary, virtual field trip

Web site, word wall

Xylograph-wood engraving or other artistic rendering

Yearbook or similar type documentary

Z to A or A to Z alphabet-type presentation

Assessment reports how well you taught and the conditions in which the learning occurred. In addition, assessment can provide insights about the relevance and appropriateness of the lesson within a unit of learning, grade level, or particular group of students. Assessment is more than a test score to record in your grade book and send home on a report card.

Like teaching methods, assessment techniques are unlimited. Select a variety of alternative assessments that fit assignments authentically and help connect the learning to the real world. For example, to learn the weekly spelling words, your students could spell the words aloud to a partner; they could write the words on paper or with markers, on the board with chalk, or on an overhead transparency; you could organize a spelling bee; they could write words on the computer and use spell-check for feedback; they could teach another student how to spell and use the new words; they could select which word is spelled either correctly or incorrectly in a sentence or story; the students could write the sentences and stories themselves and exchange papers with one another; they could use the words in a sentence, story, or conversation. Be thoughtful and inventive.

Develop Scoring Rubrics

Checklists (lists of behaviors or traits observed or not observed) and rating scales (degree to which behaviors or traits are observed) facilitate the assessment and evaluation processes (Arter & McTighe, 2001, Borich, 2004). By using rubrics or scoring guides, you identify the characteristics of an assignment, project, or performance and how the grade will be determined. Both students and parents appreciate such detailed information. The mystery is taken out of grading as it becomes more objective. Students can be involved in creating the rubrics and can self-assess their work based on the identified criteria. There are two approaches to consider. First, scoring can be holistic, giving an overall evaluation of the process and outcomes. Or scoring may be analytic, based on specific, identified behaviors or traits in which the pertinent skills and knowledge of a lesson or unit are reviewed and assessed. Many teachers like to use both approaches particularly with units of learning. You will also find that rubrics enable you to grade student work more quickly.

Decide which sort of assessment and scoring guide fits your purpose, your students, the time, the situation, etc. A wealth of ideas is available to provide you and your students with valuable and necessary feedback, advance the learning, and prepare your students for future grade levels and (yes!) standardized testing. Let assessment be your friend!

GIVE STUDENTS CHOICES IN EXPRESSION

One area that teachers overlook frequently is giving their students choices for expressing their learning. Too many teachers facilitate lessons that ask all students to produce exactly the same response or answer. This expectation may apply to some learning such as pronouncing a word or calculating an equation. Yet even words are pronounced differently according to their context or how they are used. And equations can be solved in many different ways; thinking through the process is just as powerful as calculating the solution. These are essential discussions to have in all classrooms to promote higher order and critical thinking.

When you are developing a lesson, instead of identifying a single outcome, consider several different outcomes or allowing your students to construct their own outcomes. You and your students could generate a list of ideas and post it on the wall. Then, when you are facilitating the learning and it is time to select an outcome, you and your students are ready to pick one. For language arts, each student could select a different way to write a book report. For math, each student could use a different way to group manipulatives. For science, each student could describe a different way to investigate an unknown. For social studies, each student could probe a different issue related to a social concern.

The choices for English language learners and special needs students may require additional support. You may decide to include a word bank or allow for drawings or other visual representations, outlines, or graphic organizers. Some students may also need additional time. Special needs students may need individual assistance or assistive technology.

By providing students some choice, you will realize several benefits. First, you have empowered your students to take charge of their own learning. They will be quite impressed that they have this freedom and responsibility. Second, your students will learn much more than you could ever prepare or imagine. When they share their learning with one another, you and your students gain an incredible amount of insight. Third, you will quickly discover what works with individual students and what doesn't work. You will know more about your students than you ever thought possible. You will be aware of your students' strengths and weaknesses and how to build upon each area more effectively.

DECIDE WHEN TO USE ASSESSMENTS

Assessments can be divided into three categories based on their purpose and when they are implemented: entry level or pre-assessment, progress monitoring or formative assessment, and summative assessment (Popham, 2004).

Entry level assessment or pre-assessment takes place before the initial instruction. Examples include diagnostic tests, pretests, quickwrites, and discussions that check for understanding. They reveal if students have the prerequisite knowledge and skills needed to be successful in the lesson or unit.

Progress monitoring or formative assessment takes place during instruction to see how students are progressing. Examples include checking for understanding by monitoring student work as it is completed in class or as homework. You may wish to ask questions as you present new material or have students demonstrate a new skill to verify comprehension. Student responses might be in the form of showing you answers on individual whiteboards, writing a summary at the end of a lesson for you to read, completing a graphic organizer that they submit for your review, or taking a quiz.

Summative assessment takes place at the end of a unit. Examples of summative assessment include a unit test or an alternative assessment such as a report (oral or written) or performance (debating a piece of legislation in government or playing an instrument in music). Students demonstrate mastery of several objectives in a culminating activity.

You will not be able to use all the various types of assessments for any given unit, but over the course of a semester or year, you can offer students a variety of assessment experiences. Remember, the more types you employ, the more often you give your students different opportunities to demonstrate their achievements.

BENEFIT FROM STANDARDIZED TESTING

Standardized testing, a form of summative assessment, certainly has been the focus of many discussions both in schools and throughout society. We all need to know that what is being taught is indeed being learned. We all need to know that most of the students have achieved the goals of a particular grade level or subject area and are ready for the next level. As teachers, we want to know if how we are teaching is effective and helps our students to succeed. By examining the test questions and corresponding test scores, we all can learn much about education in general, our students and their learning, as well as ourselves and our teaching.

As the data from standardized testing become available, the results will be given to you. *Criterion-referenced tests* are designed to measure what students have learned against a set of standards (criteria) such as the district objectives. Your district may have benchmark and/or semester exams. You receive specific feedback on identified objectives from this kind of evaluation. You will see how well your students did and whether any gaps or misconceptions exist that you will need to address. This information on your students will enable you to identify areas for reteaching.

The other type of information you will receive is from the *norm-referenced tests* that are currently receiving much national attention. (They are being used as the basis for school accountability.) These tests measure students against like students, usually across the nation. For example, the achievement of a second-semester "Grade X" student in your school is compared to the achievement of all second-semester "Grade X" students who took the test at that time. You will receive information on how well students did on various tasks included in the test; however, information from the task analysis tends to be general rather than specific. Also, these tests are highly dependent on reading ability, which can be problematic. Unfortunately, there is often a lag time of weeks or months between the date the test is submitted for scoring and the date the received results are shared with teachers.

Some states and school districts expect their teachers to allocate blocks of time each day to preparing for the norm-referenced tests (Abrams & Madaus, 2003). Some schools have adopted specialized programs geared simply to improving test scores. These approaches all have some benefit. Schools that do not show predetermined levels of achievement are subjected to various regulations mandated by law. These high-stake outcomes force schools and teachers to take rigorous measures to ensure success.

We suggest that you listen closely to your school principals and colleagues. Note the attitudes and concerns expressed within the neighborhood and community. Use the standardized testing and scores to your advantage to make improvements in your teaching and your students' learning.

Check your district and school calendars for dates of mandated standardized testing. You may be required to conduct pre- and post-testing of grade level skills at the beginning and end of each year along with incorporating various forms of progress monitoring throughout the year. Some assessments are given to the entire class at one time; others are given individually. Principals will guide you closely in these processes.

USE A VARIETY OF TEACHING STRATEGIES

Effective lessons begin with a check of prior knowledge and experiences. You might discover immediately that your students have mastered what you're planning to teach or that they are far from ready. Ask your students how they like to learn and how they like teachers to teach. Not only will they tell you their preferences, they will tell you what they don't like (even if you don't ask them).

"Don't make everyone do the same thing all the time. Give us time to do stuff by ourselves."

—Oliver, age 8, Grade 2

Here is a list to fan the flames of interest.

Table 6.5   Teaching Strategies to Engage the Learner

1. Challenge the students to become actively involved.	Develop interviews, plays, or simulations of events; produce projects such as journals, books, newspapers, displays, or research-related products; write a jingle, an advertisement, or a song. For a math role-play, use an algebra problem in a real-world setting. For social studies, make a magazine on the community. In geography, students can write songs to describe environments and cultures they have studied. Students with limited English language skills tend to be more comfortable working in small-group situations. Their peers will help them learn new words and use them fluently.
2. Stimulate higher level student thinking.	Teach higher order thinking skills; ask open-ended questions. Pose situations (What if . . . ? How else could . . . ?) or problems in which students will have to analyze, synthesize, and evaluate information individually and in small groups. Results from discussions can be presented to the whole class. Give students plenty of time to formulate answers. Remember: reflective thinkers need plenty of time.
3. Be dramatic.	Exaggerate your gestures and tone of voice for emphasis; use your voice to its greatest potential. Learn a magic trick; dress in a costume to create an effect. Demonstrate your excitement in the subject.
4. Decorate creatively.	Change your room; rearrange the furniture; create new bulletin boards. Turn your room into a museum by bringing in artifacts or pictures. Maybe you can bring in lamps to transform the lighting. Present a new, unexpected atmosphere, so students begin to wonder what will happen next.
5. Illustrate your subject.	Use diagrams, charts, pictures, and slides; create your own artwork or cartoons; bring in samples and models. Demonstrate: visual aids are especially important in working with English

learners. These students are often familiar with the concepts you are discussing but may not recognize the terms you use. Students with disabilities and struggling readers will also benefit from the visual references.

6. Instigate questions.
Bring in a big box or bag, and clear away the space around it. Put a question mark on the front. Let the students guess what is in it. Surprise them with an interesting object. Or, present a problem to be solved. Go on a "mystery" walk with a surprise at the end. Use inquiry as a method of teaching.

7. Inscribe thought-provoking quotations.
Questions or statements can be posed for students' reactions. They can serve as the basis of a journal entry, a brief discussion, or a way to divide the class into teams (based on student responses). Students can be given the responsibility for providing the "quotation of the day" or the "quotations of the week."

8. Introduce variety.
Plan for a "change of pace" activity. For example, assign each student a famous person to research, and provide a biography of the person. Take turns letting the rest of the students ask questions to find the identity of the person. Schedule brief reports throughout the month. Set up a round-robin or debate schedule. Use cooperative learning strategies. Have students give a brief talk on their lives as a student in your class and videotape their performances to play back for the class. Not only do students enjoy seeing themselves on tape, but the tape can be used periodically for review. Also, it provides feedback to students on their communication skills.

9. Integrate the disciplines.
No subject, such as English/language arts, has to stand alone as a separate entity. Integrate learning objectives logically and creatively to combine many different content areas, including specials. Bring in artwork associated with your topic. Play related music for the students. Or better yet, have your student musicians play for the class. Seek out teachers from different areas who are interested in joining in collaborative efforts.

(Continued)

Table 6.5 (Continued)

10. Incorporate carefully planned games.	Prepare questions and answers in advance for a game of Jeopardy or tic-tac-toe. Try baseball, where correct answers move a player around a diamond, or football, where correct answers advance a player 10 yards down a field. If you have a behaviorally responsible class, you can even play volleyball with a Nerf ball, where the right to serve is earned by correctly answering a question. A simulated Pictionary game will serve to reinforce vocabulary words. Students can play as an entire class or in teams of four. The latter, of course, will be noisy, but as you circulate around the room, you will see that the level of involvement will be quite high. Games are excellent ways to review material and reinforce knowledge.
11. Invite guest speakers and parents to your room to share their real-life experiences.	Encourage students to find people who are especially interesting and can talk about how a particular subject relates to their lives. We have seen how classes become meaningful to students when they interact with a speaker. Ask parents and community members to share their careers, hobbies, travels, cultural heritages, and so forth. Bring the real world into your classroom, so students can relate on a personal level.
12. Initiate correspondence.	Arrange for a pen pal for your class or for each student. Pen pals can be in your own school, at another school in your district, or at a school in another part of the country or the world. Many students are successfully communicating with pen pals through e-mail. The Peace Corps will match a teacher with a Peace Corps volunteer through its program called World Wise Schools.
13. Use multiple resources.	Bring in library books and CDs as well as video clips (prescreened for relevant and appropriate content). Arrange for students to go on "virtual field trips," such as to Colonial Williamsburg. Contact museums and universities to see if they have "traveling trunks" of artifacts that they will loan. Having material available at different levels will help meet the varying abilities of your students.

DETERMINE INDIVIDUAL, PARTNER, AND GROUP ACTIVITIES

Some children enjoy working in groups, while others like to work alone. Different groupings should be facilitated. You may want to assign group members based on their diversity and learning needs, or you may decide to have homogeneous groups and change group membership periodically so that all students have a chance to work with and get to know each other. For some activities, the class may participate as a whole; for other activities, partner work may be most appropriate; and the third structure is to have students work individually.

Another approach is to use a combination of groupings with differentiated learning, that is, having students work on different tasks related to a given objective according to their abilities where some work alone and some work with others (Tomlinson, 1999). This is an effective way of meeting the needs of all students in your class. In particular, it provides a structure for gifted students to work on challenging content at their own pace.

"I like working in groups and making things with other people. Last year we made erupting volcanoes."

—Kim, age 11, Grade 5

LET STUDENTS TEACH ONE ANOTHER

Here is one of the most important secrets we can share with you: the best way to learn is to teach. So let your students do it! Incorporate opportunities for your students to teach one another in your classroom.

Reflections from a first-year teacher . . .

I was assigned to teach a third grade class where most of the students read at a second grade level. I needed to improve the reading levels drastically to help my students understand third grade content and to get ready for fourth grade. I knew that we couldn't do this if I taught everyone everything, so I decided to let my students teach one another as much as possible. I divided the class into cooperative learning groups, wrote assignments on cards, and

let groups choose cards. They could select a way to express their
learning from a chart we created. Then each group taught the rest
of the class. The reading and comprehension levels increased
steadily, and the students were enthusiastic all year. Doing this
allowed me to concentrate my efforts on helping students learn
how to learn rather than on telling them what to learn.

You can also coordinate your schedule with other teachers in
your own grade level or another grade level to establish learning partners. You and your students will greatly enjoy and benefit from these
partnerships. Identify a learning purpose and outline the processes.
Find a time that fits both teachers' schedules. Some teachers set up
regular partnerships like reading or study buddies between two different grade levels such as first grade and fifth grade. Frequently,
there is more cooperation and less competition with this large span
between grade levels. One teacher we know calls these events Friday
Friends. The older student serves as a positive role model for the
younger student and instills future excitement about schooling.

"We worked with students in other grades and classes.
I especially liked reading to the Kindergarteners."

—Curtis, age 11, Grade 5

You can organize learning activities with multiple classes.
Another teacher we know plans his school year so his students present to every other class in his grade level and at least once to every
other grade level. He feels that learning improves substantially when
his students prepare and share their work with peers. He finds that
peer interaction and feedback are more important to his students
than teacher feedback in terms of increasing thoroughness and stimulating creativity.

ALLOCATE TIME TO PLAN AND PREPARE

It may appear that experienced teachers wing it without much preparation. They draw from their experiences and can make last-minute
adjustments responsibly. You cannot wing it. Plan meticulously.

Use either the detailed or the quick and easy lesson plan format for every lesson.

Try practicing your teaching privately in the classroom after the students have gone home. Doing this allows you to see if you have created the proper learning environment, collected all of the necessary materials and supplies, aligned the right assessments, and ensured a smooth flow. You might even think about your lessons in terms of how an observer would perceive the lesson.

We encourage you to be as thorough as time permits in writing your initial lesson plans. For some activities, you will want to be very complete, perhaps even scripting what you want to say. For others, a brief outline will suffice. You may be able to follow a lesson plan from another source, such as the teacher's resource kit for your textbook, a plan you received from another teacher, or one you found on the Internet. Sometimes you will be able to attach an already developed lesson to the form you use; however, most likely you will have to make adjustments for your students. As time goes on, you will become more efficient in developing your plans.

KEEP STUDENTS ACTIVELY ENGAGED . . .

If there is one bottom line for effective instruction and assessment, it is keeping the students actively engaged in their learning. This does not mean giving them busy work just to keep them occupied. You have to plan and prepare the instruction mindfully, aligning curriculum and assessment based on your grade level curriculum and your students' needs and interests. The learning must focus on your students—not on your teaching.

Staying actively engaged can involve sitting still and listening, reading a book, writing a paper, and watching a presentation or video. Ask your students a question and wait quietly. Inside your head, count to ten. Then ask students to write a quick response before anyone talks. These prompts encourage some of the most productive kinds of active engagement.

Today's elementary school students like to be entertained and to have the entertainment change frequently. Too often, they expect someone else to tell them what to do. Your job is to shift their passiveness to engagement that is purposeful, productive, and positive.

Suggested Activities

1. Interview several students, and ask them how they best like to learn in school. Then interview teachers, and ask them how they best like to teach. Compare and contrast their answers.

2. Ask to see a veteran teacher's planning book as a model for variety of activities and time spent on instruction and assessment.

3. Evaluate the advantages of both the detailed and the quick-and-easy lesson plan formats given in the chapter.

4. Consider your classroom from the perspective of parents/guardians. What will they see happening and on display when they walk in?

CHAPTER SEVEN

Establishing Routines and Management

One morning during my first year of teaching, I awoke with no voice. I felt fine; I just couldn't talk. Nothing extraordinary was planned for the day, so I decided to let the students be the teachers. I wrote a message on the overhead transparency explaining the situation with the details of my plan. I would select two name sticks from the can, and those two students would be the teachers for 30 minutes. Since I taught 300 minutes a day, and there were 20 students in the room, the time worked out evenly. All of the students knew exactly what to do all day long. This gave me the chance both to observe and to participate silently. I was impressed how smoothly the class functioned and how well the students interacted with one another. During math, the principal popped in and marveled at our success. After that day, our class became a more coherent community of learners, taking more responsibility for everything we did.

From this example, you realize that this new teacher had successfully modeled and positively reinforced the expectations associated with classroom routines. The students became the teachers, reviewing the content and demonstrating the processes for each subject area. We can imagine that putting the students in charge and shifting the center of attention from teacher to students greatly inspired student cooperation. If this experiment were successful, they would probably get to do it again. Your job, then, is to establish a system to keep your students, and yourself, knowledgeable and energized about what is going on in your classroom.

Classroom management is probably the number one concern of all new (and many veteran) teachers. Study after study reveals that good classroom management is vital for effective teaching and student learning to occur (Marzano, Marzano, & Pickering, 2003). The first step is to demonstrate expectations and establish routines that you will be comfortable implementing (Bevel & Jordan, 2003).

FAMILIARIZE STUDENTS WITH SCHOOL FACILITIES

In an earlier chapter, we mentioned showing your students around the school and the use of facilities on the first day of school. Many of the procedures regarding use of the facilities will need to be revisited frequently and in more detail throughout the year. Students benefit greatly when they practice procedures under your supervision until the procedures become natural and routine (Marzano, 2003). Here are some of the more important areas to consider.

Drinking Fountains. Some of you will have drinking fountains in your classrooms, and some of you will access fountains down the hall. Decide when students can use the fountains and how long students can stay at the fountains. If the fountain is in your room, you also have to decide what supplies you need near the fountain and to monitor who is responsible for cleaning up the area at the end of the day. You may want to add paper towels to your student school supply list.

More students will want to use the fountain if they have been playing a game on the playground or in the gym. If this is the case, it may be better to have students sit at their desks before anyone uses the fountain, so you can supervise the use in an organized manner. You can dismiss groups of students to get drinks quickly in the classroom. If the fountain is located in the hall, you will have to organize getting drinks differently, coordinating with other teachers whose students are assigned to the same drinking fountain. These procedures apply whenever your class returns to the room as a whole group or following an active in-class group event.

Throughout the day, you can allow students to get drinks at their own discretion if the fountain is located in the room. If the fountain is located in the hall, you need to establish a pass system that applies to any student leaving the classroom for any reason.

Restrooms. In most schools, the restrooms are located off a central hall adjacent to the classroom with separate facilities for girls and boys. However, in some schools, the restrooms are located off the classroom; sometimes there are separate facilities for each gender and sometimes there is just one. Again, routines are essential when many or all students need to use the restroom, such as when they enter the classroom as a whole class at the beginning of the school day and when they return from specials, lunch, or recess. You may need to allow for the whole class to leave the classroom and walk to the restrooms, lining up in the hallway before and after using the facilities. If the drinking fountain is nearby, you can include getting drinks during this procedure. Standing in the hall with your students allows you to supervise them closely.

Hall Passes. Throughout the day, students will need to leave the room at various times. We strongly urge you to design a pass system. Your school may have a schoolwide plan that you need to follow; this is good time to check the faculty handbook and talk with your grade level colleagues. Perhaps you would like students to place a name card from one hook or pocket to another indicating that someone is out of the classroom. Or, you may want cards for each student that are placed in corresponding pockets when they leave the room to go to the main office, health office, restroom, library, special classes, or other locations. Some schools want students to carry a tag with them when they leave the classroom. The tag indicates what classroom the students are from and where they are going.

Secrets from a first-year teacher . . .

I went to a building supply store and asked for some countertop samples with holes punched in them. I put four cup holder hooks in the wall near the classroom door. Above two sets of hooks, I placed a sign that read "Boys IN and Boys OUT," and above the other two sets of hooks, I placed a sign that read "Girls IN and Girls OUT." I wrote the word "Boy" on one of the countertop samples and the word "Girl" on the other sample to create passes. I placed the passes underneath the IN signs indicating that all boys and girls were in the classroom. Then I explained to the students that at appropriate times, if the pass is in the IN location, they could move it to the OUT position and leave the classroom to use the restroom or get a drink. The passes stayed in the room and clean. By using the hooks and looking around the classroom, I could detect who had left the room right away.

DEMONSTRATE USES OF CLASSROOM FEATURES

Every classroom includes several features such as pencil sharpeners, tissue boxes, and waste baskets. You have already thought carefully about where to place these features so students can get to them quickly and easily, while not causing a distraction to other students or to you.

Pencil Sharpener: Teachers frequently have to remind some of their students that they are going to the pencil sharpener too often or spending too much time there. Going to the pencil sharpener gives students a reason to move around and think about something besides their assignments. Become aware of who is going, how often, and why this is happening.

Coat Hooks, Sinks, Tissue Dispensers. These same concerns related to off-task behavior apply to other classroom features, such as the classroom sink and coat hooks, and to other locations either in or out of the classroom where students can go independently. Another secret: provide adequate time and space for students to get ready to do their work while increasing time and efficiency in order to avoid their wasting time wandering around the room.

SHOW STUDENTS HOW TO ACCESS MATERIALS

You will have set up areas around the room for storage of supplies and learning centers. Indicate to students how and when they may access these areas. You want to be clear with your students about which areas they can access without permission and which areas require the teacher's permission and/or assistance.

Materials. Sometimes you will want to distribute supplies as you are giving instructions. These may be supplies that are readily available or special items relevant to one particular lesson. If you have student helpers, you can ask your paper monitor to help you. If there is an abundance of materials, you can ask the substitute helper to help too. You should not spend your time distributing materials; you should concentrate on implementing the lesson and managing the class.

If you keep frequently used materials readily available in baskets, students can access them individually as supplies are needed.

Most elementary school students will not abuse this privilege; plus, you need to help your students learn to make wise choices and become responsible for their own behaviors.

Learning Centers. Some teachers use centers as extensions for students who complete their assignments and need more to do. Keep in mind that, with this system, some students may never have the opportunity to go to centers, as they may never finish their assignments early. (And some students may rush through assignments to get to centers they enjoy.) In other situations, teachers schedule a specific time during the day for centers and expect all students to go to the centers and complete the assignments at each one. Uncompleted center assignments may become homework. You have to decide how to organize your centers based on your curriculum, your students, you, and your school. Many new teachers are not comfortable using centers at the beginning of their first year and wait until the second semester.

Fragile Items. Finally, there are materials that students must access carefully, such as science kits or audiovisual equipment. You should supervise their access closely, as these supplies are often expensive, breakable, or need to last a long time.

STAY POSITIVE AND PATIENT

During the first few days, maybe even the first few weeks of school, you may feel like you're stuck in the movie "Ground Hog Day." It may seem like you have to repeat instructions and directions frequently. Relax; this is normal. Students need gentle reminders of the classroom routines you are establishing for them.

As you start a new school year, your students are the products of three overwhelming forces: their families, their summer vacations, and their previous teachers. First, every family has a different set of expectations, different ways of doing things and expressing themselves, and different guidelines. What is allowed in one home is not permitted in another and vice versa. Certainly, what is allowed in most homes is not permitted at school.

Second, your students are returning to school after their summer vacations. That probably meant modified routines and reduced structures;

few of your students have been reading, writing, or calculating on a daily basis. We would guess that they have not been going to bed early either. Third, your students have acquired their school behaviors from the interactions allowed by their previous teachers. By the time older students enter school, they are the products of many different kinds of teachers' expectations.

Our advice is to smile, be yourself, and give your students a chance. Yes, you will have to revisit your behavior expectations frequently as you get the year started. You may even decide to modify them along the way, requiring you to start all over again. Stay positive and patient. Your actions are modeling an incredible image to your students.

EXPLAIN SCHOOL DISCIPLINE POLICIES

Most elementary schools have established schoolwide discipline policies (Canter, 1992). Usually, these policies entail how students are expected to act when entering the school, playing on the playgrounds, moving through the hallways, eating in the cafeteria, and attending classes other than in their regular classrooms. They provide for the orderly and safe movement of children. Explain these discipline policies to prevent behavior problems (Boynton & Boynton, 2005).

"In the morning we sit at lunch tables, and we pick a book and read it. When the bell rings, we stop, and then the teacher puts down an orange cone and calls the second graders to leave and make a line. Then we go to the classroom."

—Fernando, age 8, Grade 2

Examples of elementary schoolwide policies include

- Do your best at all times, in all places, and with all people.
- Use respectful, school appropriate words and language.
- Walk in the halls and rooms at all times.
- Keep your hands and feet to yourself.
- Keep your voice low or silent.
- Enter the school through assigned doors (e.g., by classroom, not through the office).

- Go to the main office, cafeteria, media center, technology lab, and health office only with your teacher's permission.
- Play only on your assigned areas of the playground.
- Do not chew gum or bring gum to school.
- Do not bring weapons to school.

Examples of schoolwide consequences may include

First offense: discussion with teacher

Second offense: time out from classroom or playground

Third offense: discussion with principal

Fourth offense: discussion with parent

Fifth offense: time out from school or school event

Show your students exactly what you mean and want. If one of your expectations is for them to quietly raise their hands to be called on to talk, then demonstrate to students how to raise a hand without waving it obnoxiously when someone else is talking. The secret is to repeat the expected action naturally and frequently. Tell your students exactly what they are not allowed to do, not allowed to say, or places they are not allowed to go. Give your students genuine reasons that they should not do something, say something, or go to unauthorized places, reasons emphasizing health, safety, cooperation, and care. We recommend that you state your expectations positively, as if misbehaviors are not going to actually happen. Avoid talking to your students as if you don't trust them and can't wait to punish them. Reassure your students that you care about them, you are there to help them remember expectations, and you will give them some time to act as you and everyone at the school expects them to behave.

"My teacher says, 'Little friends, don't change your colors . . . Green means good. Yellow means 5 minutes [sitting in at recess]. Orange is 10 minutes. Red means the principal's office.'"

—Jordyn, age 5, Kindergarten

As a visual reminder to help students monitor their behaviors, many teachers place their students' names on clips and move the clips from one color designation to another depending on the students' behaviors, such as green light, yellow light, red light. Students immediately can see the consequences of their behaviors yet know they can move back toward the green if they are good again.

DECIDE CLASSROOM PROCEDURES COLLABORATIVELY

As mentioned in our discussion about class rules on the first day, it is more productive, and more fun, if you decide some classroom procedures collaboratively (DeVries & Zan, 2003).

If your class lines up on the playground in the mornings before school, you and your students can decide together the order students should line up. Your class may decide it simply doesn't matter. Your class may decide there should be a new line leader designated weekly, as shown on the helper chart, who collects the playground equipment and leads the class into the building or classroom. Your class may decide that the best citizens for the week get to be last ones in line, so they can play longer.

You can build a sense of community with your students when you involve them in making procedural decisions. They can help you create the list of helpers. This empowerment communicates a sense of authority and responsibility. Students shift their beliefs and begin thinking about the classroom as theirs rather than yours. This shift will help make them more conscientious around others and things. You will reap incredible benefits for taking the time to make decisions collaboratively.

DISCUSS CONSEQUENCES

Naturally, with every expectation you have to be ready with consequences. The consequences include rewards for compliance and punishments for lack of compliance. Your reward system needs to include both planned and spontaneous rewards, ranging from the formal to the informal. Planned formal rewards may include schoolwide annual awards given at school assemblies for attendance, grades, academic and extracurricular accomplishments, displays, competitions, good citizenship, and so on. Assemblies may be held weekly, monthly, every quarter or semester, or at the end of the year. Formal awards become part of the school's traditions and culture. These are important events to share with parents and families. Many teachers have happy memories of their own childhood school awards.

Planned rewards are appropriate within grade level or individual classrooms too. If you expect your class to be seated, quiet, and ready for class following a certain signal (the bell rings or you make an announcement), then you need to acknowledge compliant behaviors. This can be verbal praise with or without some type of tangible reward.

Spontaneous rewards are powerful as well. In one classroom, we saw that the teacher had set up plastic jars in the center of each group of five desks. When the teacher prompted students to make transitions, she would call out something like, "The first group who is ready for math earns five stars in their jar." The teacher had a large box of Styrofoam packing pieces in the shapes of stars. After all (or most) of the groups were settled for math, the teacher would look around and reward the first group by placing five stars in the jar. When a group had filled its jar, the group earned a bigger reward, such as pencil eraser tops or extra time at learning centers. This teacher also used the stars in the jars as punishment. If groups were misbehaving and had been warned, the teacher would remove a specified number of stars. You can modify this type of system by adding or taking away points or stickers that individuals or groups accumulate on a board or chart.

> "When we are good, they give us stickers. Sometimes we get a longer recess!"
>
> —Kia, age 11, Grade 5

Many elementary schools have established discipline policies that all teachers are expected to follow in their classrooms. This approach is thought to communicate a unified system more clearly to the students. So if a student misbehaves outside of the classroom, a single record is maintained. Obviously, there are strengths and weaknesses to such an approach. Yes, there is only one record, so a playground teaching assistant can tell the classroom teacher if a child misbehaves. However, this approach may place the classroom teacher in the awkward position of following up with students for misbehaviors not experienced during the classroom teacher's supervision. The faculty and staff at a school adopting a schoolwide plan must agree to inform and support one another.

If you are responsible for developing your own set of consequences, then you need to consider what misbehaviors you simply cannot tolerate, the appropriate actions you will take, and your ability to apply the consequences consistently. Try not to develop a system that is too complicated or time consuming. Be sure you communicate your system clearly to your students, their families, and your colleagues.

REINFORCE FREQUENTLY

Several major challenges await you. First, you have to remember to positively reinforce desired behavior frequently (Boynton & Boynton, 2005). That means you have to show that you are pleased when students do and say what you presume they should do and say. If you do not positively reinforce desired behavior, students may not know for sure that they did what they should have done. And, they may not continue practicing the desired behavior. Second, you must be sincere about this. For example, a student pushes her chair under her desk when she gets up to go to the restroom. If you are nearby, thank the girl for remembering to do this in a manner that sincerely communicates appreciation of her consideration of others.

Third, you want to positively reinforce desired behaviors using "I" messages. In this case, you could say, "I appreciate your pushing in your chair; that is thoughtful of other students." Finally, positive reinforcement needs to be intermittent. That means it is random and inconsistent. This randomness is what makes gambling so successful. People never know when they are going to win, so they keep playing. The same is true about your words of praise. Your learners will simply glow and be as good as gold if they receive positive reinforcement from time to time. Your challenge simply is to remember to use it and not take desired behavior for granted. As one teacher says, "I try to catch 'em being good."

DISCIPLINE FAIRLY

Carefully think through the consequences for misbehaviors and the discipline that will accompany misbehaviors in your classroom. Create a list of consequences that matches the schoolwide discipline plan. You might want to insert an extra warning or two.

First offense: discussion with teacher

1st Warning: discussion with teacher and name on a list

2nd Warning: more serious discussion and check next to name

Second offense: time out from classroom or playground

3rd Warning: writing short explanation of misbehavior and anticipated changes

Third offense: discussion with principal

Discipline is tricky because you have to individualize every situation based on reasons for misbehaviors and past offenses while still weighing the severity of the misbehavior and being fair. During your first year, keep your expectations as clear as possible. Listen closely and weigh your decisions carefully as you monitor your reinforcement and reward system cautiously. However, you will soon discover that exceptions occur and rules have to be broken. When this happens, you have to discuss the situations with your students, so they understand your reasoning. And, at times, you may have to say that you have made a decision because you are the teacher with no more explanation. In some situations, you must maintain confidentiality and silence. Whew! It isn't easy.

And watch out! Our experience tells us that most teachers are more likely to notice and punish misbehaviors than to notice and reward desired behaviors. Perhaps it is human nature to be disturbed by what is wrong rather than appreciating what is right. Be aware of your attitudes and approaches. You may discover that you are picking on some students and letting other students slide by.

"Don't make everyone lose recess when a few people misbehave. Take the bad kids to the principal and leave us out of it."

—Duane, age 9, Grade 3

There are more than two dozen different models of classroom discipline, each with its own perspective. We feel it is imperative that you give serious thought to your philosophical beliefs on this subject and to how you want to manage your classroom.

Be proactive rather than waiting for trouble to start. Students will benefit when you provide a supportive structure that is implemented fairly and consistently.

BUILD COMMUNITY WITH CLASS MEETINGS

The goal is to have students refer to the classroom as "our room" not "your" room. You can begin by modeling this language and avoid saying "my classroom" or posting signs that read "my rules." The more you guide and support appropriate ways of acting in and outside the classroom, the more students will show active ownership of the routines and responsibility for their classroom (Kohn, 1999).

One of the most effective ways to build a learning community is to hold a class meeting on a regular basis. Earlier we mentioned a typical morning meeting during which you can talk about current events, make announcements, and preview the day's agenda and assignments. A class meeting is different, and we suggest you conduct your class meetings at another time during the day, such as immediately before or after lunch, when you have plenty of time and all of your students are in the classroom. (Some students may leave the class to attend other classes. A valuable secret for building a classroom community is to include all students in class meetings.)

During a class meeting, you and your students address classroom or school issues that need discussion. Issues might include such topics as ongoing or escalating discipline problems, upcoming changes in the schedule, major events or fundraisers with feedback sent to the principal, counselor, PTO, or other individuals. Classroom meetings teach student responsibility (Marzano, Marzano, & Pickering, 2003). You want to demonstrate how a typical class meeting will be run early in the school year, using a safe subject such as how to keep the playground clean or how to check out books in the library.

Begin by asking students to put away all of their books and materials. Students should give the discussion their undivided attention. We suggest that you serve as leader of the first few meetings. Then you can decide if you want to select or elect a class meeting leader based on what you consider developmentally appropriate for your students. Many teachers compromise and serve as coleader, so they can model and reinforce both effective leadership and active participation. Taking turns, each student is given a chance to speak.

The class meeting should open with the leader stating the reason for the meeting in a neutral tone. Some classes meet regularly even when there is no urgent new business. Some classes take notes and begin with the reading of the minutes. This can be particularly helpful when the class is addressing an ongoing problem.

MODEL GENUINE CARE AND CONCERN

The most important part of establishing routines for effective classroom management is to show your students that you care about them (Noddings, 1992). Students like teachers who are firm, fair, and consistent. They want teachers to be in control of the class, set boundaries, and promote mutual respect. Most students realize that their teachers honestly care about them and want them to be successful academically and socially. Based on these beliefs about their teachers, students will do work even when they do not personally value it or find the task relevant.

> "I like when [my teachers] take time to talk to us as people and listen to our ideas . . . They talk to us. They help us work through our problems and give us time to understand the situation and help make the decisions."
>
> —Typasha, age 9, Grade 3

You are an extremely important role model in all that you do and say—formally and informally. Think back to some of your own elementary school teachers and the images they have left with you. You want to create positive images that will stay with your students for a lifetime, as they become older students, young adults, parents, maybe even teachers. You will make a difference in every child's life.

BE SURE THE CLASSROOM IS A SHARED SPACE . . .

Although you are responsible for organizing your classroom and establishing routines, you must quickly change it into a space that belongs to everyone—your students and their families. Your goal is to create an environment conducive to learning and living that is shared and enjoyed by all. You and your students will spend an enormous amount of time together in this space; it must belong to all of you.

Suggested Activities

1. As you walk through several classrooms, observe the different rules that are posted. Think about which ones you feel are the most meaningful and helpful.

2. Observe how different teachers implement classroom management. How do teachers maintain a sense of fairness and equity?

3. Visit a classroom and record all the ways the teacher positively reinforces behavior. Compare your list with a colleague's list.

4. Keep a list with every student's name. As the day goes along, jot down a nice comment you made to each one. Repeat this behavior from time to time to monitor your behavior.

CHAPTER EIGHT

Valuing Cultural Diversity

W ho are the students in your classroom? How did their families come to live in the neighborhood? How does each family contribute to the social, economic, and political structure of the community and our country? How will you ensure that the cultural diversity of every child is understood, practiced, and appreciated? How will you make the process of valuing cultural diversity authentic and natural in your daily academic and social activities? All these questions motivate teachers.

The United States is a nation that has grown from the original inhabitants of our lands to the expansive communities of diverse populations we know today. Combined with the members of indigenous Native American Indian tribes, many different people now form the nation, people who have emigrated (and continue to emigrate) from countries all around the world. We no longer refer to U.S. citizens as a "melting pot" of individuals all becoming one, assimilating into a single way of thinking, believing, speaking, and acting. Today, people honor and embrace the wealth of cultural diversity in metaphoric terms such as a "tossed salad," a "turning kaleidoscope," or a "pieced-together quilt."

Children must be taught that all members of our society make valuable contributions to both our individual and shared existence, fulfilling our sense of well-being and accomplishment (Oakes & Lipton, 2003). Our past, present, and future populations are our greatest assets. Teachers play one of the most important roles in nurturing these vital resources.

As we move into the twenty-first century, individuals of all ages, in all stages, and from every country find themselves interacting

111

with many different kinds of people. We hear news about events occurring in our own neighborhoods and far away, stories that impact our daily living. We eat foods and use products originating from many different countries. We travel to every country and conduct business worldwide on a regular basis. We all seem to be interconnected, and, whether we live next door or in the next country, each member of the global society offers valuable contributions that benefit everyone else. American children are multicultural representatives of the world; they must be prepared to live, work, and play as the adults of tomorrow in an interdependent global society.

BECOME ACQUAINTED WITH FAMILIES

All children enter school as unique individuals shaped by their families, friends, and society. Families come in many different packages; there may be only one parent or one primary parent. There may be two, three, four, or more parents and grandparents. Parents, as well as grandparents, may be younger or older than you might expect. The parents may have a range of sexual orientations and intimate relationships. Some students live with guardians. There may be brothers and sisters with various parents or guardians all living together in one home. Children may have to divide their family time and personal energies between or among various homes during the school week or over the weekend. Some children are homeless. For some children and teachers, these configurations work quite smoothly, and everyone copes easily with the required transitions. For other children, the situations are unsettled and more difficult. The challenges affect more than the children immediately connected to the situations; the children's friends and teachers are aware of them too.

Today's families operate in many different ways. One or both parents may work either out of the home or from the home. Work hours may not coincide with children's school hours. Work may take adults far from home for short or long periods of time. Adults of all ages are enrolled in schools, colleges, institutes, and universities for adult education or advanced training. In some homes, no one is working for a wage. Children may or may not understand the kind of work that their parents and other family members do, their family's economic status, or the distribution of wealth among family members. Some of today's children live in families with huge amounts of money and disposable incomes; some live in incredible poverty with little hope of living comfortably or altering their futures. However, most children live somewhere in the middle and have a basic awareness of their resources as well as their spending limitations.

Families place varying degrees of importance on their time and assign different priorities to specific activities and expenditures. One family may be more dedicated to school and academics; another may be more committed to family and time together. Another may be more devoted to religious activities or community endeavors. Yet another may allocate more energy to social groups or personal pursuits. The United States is a wonderful blend of all kinds of families who function on their own and among others in all kinds of ways.

Religious beliefs and practices play significant roles in many of today's families. Some families attend worship services regularly one or more times per week; their practices influence their daily lives in various ways. Religious customs and observations may regulate what children eat, wear, and say, as well as their school attendance on special days. For example, because of their religious beliefs, some children may or may not eat particular foods and wear religious clothing or jewelry on special days. Their religious backgrounds may also determine what activities they participate in. They may not be allowed to recite the Pledge of Allegiance or to participate in traditional classroom holiday celebrations. Children may be enrolled in religion classes or special events after school that place additional expectations upon their time, energies, and social interactions. Teachers need to be aware that religious affiliations may affect both the children participating in the customs as well as all the children with whom they come in contact.

Though you cannot ask direct questions, you can learn about your students, their families, and their backgrounds in ways that are easy and fun. Ask your students to write stories about their families illustrated with drawings or photographs. Stories can be exchanged during language arts, social studies, or a special sharing time such as "Show and Tell" followed by valuable question and answer sessions. You can send home a letter inviting parents to come to class and describe their family traditions, jobs, hobbies, and areas of expertise. Children love having their parents visit the classroom.

UNDERSTAND THAT EVERY CHILD IS UNIQUE AND SPECIAL

The children across the United States represent every racial and religious background and possible combination of heritage and nationality. They speak every language and dialect found around the world, regardless of the number of generations their families have been living in the United States. Children live in cities, suburbs, small towns, and rural settings; they live in houses, apartments, condos, trailer houses, and on farms.

They have all kinds of abilities, needs, and interests; they learn and express their learning in many different ways (Robins, Lindsey, Lindsey, & Terrell, 2002; Spinelli, 2002; Tomlinson, 1999). They may be well or sick, able or disabled. They wear all kinds of clothing, eat all kinds of foods, travel by all kinds of transportation, and play all kinds of games. Today's children may be highly involved in academics, sports, music, technology, community groups, or social events; they may prefer the company of a few close friends and individual pursuits. All of these characteristics greatly influence children's understanding of themselves, their interactions with one another, and their views of society.

During their formative years, children form a sense of normalcy. How they were raised prior to attending school establishes the basis for their lifelong values and personal beliefs. Most elementary school children enter school thinking that other children and families are just like them and their families. Naïvely, children expect their teachers and the school to continue the kinds of support and reinforcement that they have experienced during their preschool years, and they are surprised when they discover that other families are unlike their own. As you realize that children come from every kind of background and home that is possible, you recognize the importance of providing a sense of stability and acceptance for all children in your classrooms.

RECOGNIZE YOUR OWN
CULTURAL CHARACTERISTICS

Typically, today's teacher is Anglo, heterosexual, and married, with both adults working outside the home; she has children, lives in the suburbs, and practices strong family and Christian-Judeo religious beliefs. But these cultural characteristics do not match the cultural characteristics reflective of many of your students. There is a significant dissonance of culture between today's teachers and students. And these differences may strongly impact your success with your young learners.

You will benefit greatly by taking a little time when you begin teaching to consider how you are both similar to and different from your students, their families, and their cultures (Howard, 1999). Be honest with yourself as you reflect upon your assumptions, values, and beliefs. You may discover that your thoughts, words, and actions do not always support or communicate your intentions. You want to be sure that you exhibit respect for all of your students inclusive of their cultural characteristics, backgrounds, and lifestyles.

LEARN TO ACCEPT SIMILARITIES AND DIFFERENCES

It is important not only to notice one's race and ethnicity but also to accept and celebrate racial and ethnic similarities and differences. For many years, it was common to hear teachers make statements like, "I don't see color; I treat all of my students the very same." There was an assumed fear that to see color would indicate that one might be acting with prejudice or bias. However, today most people want to be seen for who they are. They want to be treated with respect regarding their race and ethnicity as well as their language, gender, social class, abilities, size, and other characteristics.

Each of us is composed of many different cultural characteristics that make us both similar to and different from others. We may live in the same neighborhoods but prefer wearing different styles of clothing. We may attend the same schools but speak different languages at home. We may play the same sports but follow different religions. One skin color, ethnicity, neighborhood, or religion is not better than another; it is just different. Many members of U.S. society embrace our wealth of diverse cultural characteristics.

Sadly, we have members of our society who do not agree with these statements. These people tend to think, believe, speak, or act in ways that are neither respectful nor accepting of a person who may appear to be different from themselves, or whom they perceive to be different in appearance, thinking, or behavior. This is called stereotyping, and it easily influences how we interact with one another, especially in classrooms. When we stereotype, we behave with bias, prejudice, and hate. Those who stereotype may or may not be aware of their behaviors. Some individuals who stereotype are said to display their behaviors overtly or openly. They purposely act in ways that are denigrating of others and seek to disenfranchise individuals or groups of people from equal acceptance by and participation in society.

Some individuals who stereotype tend to operate more covertly or covered up from public view; these behaviors appear less obvious and may cause more harm. People who act with prejudice covertly make decisions and enact measures that greatly impact individuals and groups, and these people act without conversation or announcement. Such decisions and measures reflect the power that members of the dominant or privileged segment of society hold (or want to control). Frequently, covert stereotyping is manifested by treating individuals or members of groups as if they did not exist or were invisible. It is essential that you be aware of your thoughts, beliefs, words, and actions about people like and unlike you and of how you acknowledge and interact with each individual.

From a new teacher . . .

I decided to help the students in my classroom understand the diversity of our nation coupled with the importance of knowing more and caring about one another in different ways. I found a bucket of small mirrors in the science closet and a pile of construction paper in the art closet and brought them to my room. I was particularly interested in finding every shade of paper that was the same as every different skin tone and eye color of my students. I purposefully removed the stark white construction paper. I assigned my students to partners of the same gender and gave each student a mirror. I asked the students to look carefully at their faces and for a long period of time. Then I asked them to look at their partners' faces the same way. I wanted them to see the colors, shapes, and placement. They could touch their partners' faces if the partner said it was okay. I wanted the students to discover that, although we think everyone is the same, everyone is different, unique, and special.

Students were asked to select pieces of construction paper that matched all the colors representing their [own] facial features. The students were shown how to tear the paper, rather than cut it with scissors, to reproduce what they saw in their mirrors. Partners asked one another to help them select the right colors and tear the right shapes. The students were astounded that what they thought did not match with what they saw.

Students wanted to tell stories about their experiences, so I dedicated the next afternoon to a multicultural education conversation. Then, we hung the self-portraits on the wall in the main hallway in time for parent conferences. The students showed their self-portraits to their parents and repeated their stories to them. Everyone was extremely impressed with this insightful natural learning experience.

TAKE TIME TO INCORPORATE MULTICULTURAL EDUCATION

Let's take a moment to distinguish multicultural education from international education and global education.

International Education focuses on learning about lands and people in countries other than the United States. It explores topics and issues related to physical and cultural geography, identifying for the learner the various features found in each country. This approach to learning about people allows students to compare the similarities and differences of people outside of the United States with those of people inside the United States. International education focuses on identification and description.

Global Education focuses on the interactions among several countries. Through global education, students explore functions—such as governmental systems, economic interactions, legal issues, and environmental concerns—that affect everyone. Global education advocates consideration of the planet as one huge community, concentrating on the existence and endurance of this community as a consequence of its members' collective strengths and interdependent vitality.

Multicultural Education. To the understanding of both international education and global education from personal and school experiences, you add the multicultural perspective, which values diversity in meeting these three goals:

1. teaching all children about themselves, all other children, and the limitless contributions by all cultures to U.S. society;

2. including all children equitably in the teaching/learning processes in pursuit of academic engagement and scholarly excellence; and

3. demonstrating genuine care and concern for the heritages and traditions of each of your students and their families.

Understanding and appreciating all cultures, particularly the cultures in one's own teaching community, requires dedicated time and energy. Begin by listening carefully to your students. When your students are provided a sense of safety and are given time to talk, they will share their stories, observations, concerns, and dreams. These rich and powerful exchanges not only inform and support the students individually and among their peers but also provide a wealth of new knowledge and insight for the teachers (Nieto, 2005).

Reflections from a new teacher . . .

> I taught at a school where approximately one-fourth of the students lived in migrant farming families. The students were enrolled at our school during the early fall and late spring, but they were gone during the rest of the school year. I learned to listen to the children and let them share their stories, their lives, with the other children. I knew that everyone's story should be valued and everyone's story becomes a part of our own story. That was over 30 years ago, and, as we all know, the migrant family and their children are still making important contributions to our society today.

Students can share during reading group discussions, literature circles, journal writing, artwork, playground games, lunchroom conversations, social studies and science discussions and debates, and so forth. Stay open, and allow those teachable moments related to cultural diversity to occur frequently and naturally.

Visit the Area Around Your School

It will benefit you to look at the area around your school to see the diversity of children who attend the school as well as the diversity of adults who work there. Drive around the neighborhood; visit the shops and investigate the local goods and services. See if you can locate the nearest park, library, and recreation center that your students and their families frequent. If you feel unsafe or uncomfortable driving around, take several colleagues with you and share the experience.

Then drive around the entire town or city. You may have been raised in the vicinity without having visited certain sections of town. You may discover neighborhoods where children live in tiny apartments or large houses; perhaps the stores are located in the fronts of office buildings or isolated in distant malls; there may be billboards written completely in Spanish or no billboards at all. Although you are a "tourist" on this first visit, try to return and become more comfortable with the neighborhood and with yourself in it. Remember that no one section of a town or city is better or worse; each one is different, and each one makes a valuable contribution to our society.

MEET MULTICULTURAL EDUCATIONAL GOALS

In order to meet the three educational goals associated with valuing cultural diversity, you need to begin learning your students' cultures by examining them multiculturally. Many students have never seen people like themselves portrayed at all (or portrayed in a positive light) in books and magazines, on posters and signs, on television and movie screens. It is almost as if they do not exist, or they exist only as negative, sinister, or comical examples. As teachers attempt to inspire their students to achieve in school, many of their students cannot begin to imagine how to fulfill an "American dream" that does not include them in the picture.

A suggestion from another new teacher . . .

> In order to know more about my students and their families multiculturally, I created a time during our morning meetings to hear about students' cultural backgrounds. Twice a week, we featured the "Student Spotlight." Students were assigned specific dates and were expected to bring photographs and artifacts. Three students were selected to ask questions of the featured student, so we could learn how to conduct a meaningful interview as well as learn more about one another. Many of my students' families expressed appreciation for my taking time to learn about the students multiculturally.

Learning about culture can be accomplished in every subject area. When you teach literacy, stories illustrative of all cultures can be read to, about, and by all children. When you teach math and science, word problems and scientific explorations situated in various cultural contexts can be presented to students. When you teach social studies, health, and the fine arts, cultural contributions can be shared by the students and their families. This is only a beginning. Suggestions to enrich and enhance curricular content are endless.

Teachers must demonstrate genuine care and concern for the heritages and traditions of each of their students and their families and for the cultures of children across the United States. These attitudes are manifested through teachers' words and actions, selection of books and materials, teaching strategies and disciplinary measures, reinforcement of classroom rules and expectations that emphasize tolerance with students, and communication with families. Care and concern must be honest and frequent.

Realization from a first-year teacher . . .

> I was not raised near anyone who practiced a different religion than my own. I thought in terms of one type of belief, and I referred to "church" for all religious activities. One day a student in my second-grade class asked me if I would like to attend a special ceremony at his temple. I didn't even know the child was a member of the temple. I suddenly realized that I was talking to my students as though there was only one type of religious practice. I drove around the community and found temples and mosques and all kinds of religious centers. I was shocked to realize that my thoughts, words, and actions left out some children when I believed in tolerance and diversity. At that point, I knew I had to change so my teaching was for all children and about all children.

BE AWARE OF GENDER BIAS

The English language is filled with gender references. During the twentieth century, many efforts were started to remove these references from our formal and informal conversations and publications. For example, we no longer use the impersonal pronoun "he" when describing any person—male or female—or the word "man" or "mankind" in reference to humans. Today we use gender-free language by speaking and writing in the plural when at all possible, as in "Students . . . their" rather than "He . . . his" or "she . . . her." (Also, teachers should not use the word "guys" to refer to both men and women, boys and girls.) We recognize that all professions can be filled by either men or women, so we no longer make presumptive and exclusive references, such as to doctors as men and nurses as women. Nor do we refer to firefighters as firemen or to postal clerks and deliverers as mailmen.

However, many of today's teachers were raised in families and taught in classrooms where males were considered dominant and treated with more privilege. And many of tomorrow's teachers may experience the same situations, particularly if today's teachers fail to ensure equity in their classrooms. Unfortunately, it comes "naturally" to many teachers to use gender-biased references. These teachers may claim that it is "how they were raised" and that they "do it without thinking." It is imperative that all teachers be aware of how they were raised and think about their selection of words. Our words shape our behaviors.

The vocabulary modeled in the classroom sends powerful messages to young learners. As they hear the words being spoken and the appropriate uses reinforced, young learners start to negotiate the differences between what they hear at home or with their peers and what they hear in school. As young learners make oral presentations and produce written products, they will strive to achieve the language patterns modeled and reinforced by their teachers.

It may be appropriate for teachers to identify specific language concerns to their students as part of the study of social studies and culture or as part of students' speaking and writing skill development. These conversations should be approached with diplomacy. Some new teachers may wince at this suggestion thinking that this is an example of being "politically correct" or "PC." Yes, you should be "PC." Try to think of "PC" as being "personally conscientious" and "professionally competent" (Howard, 1999). These charges are the responsibilities of every teacher and every human being.

NOTICE TEACHING ZONES OF PROXIMITY

In addition to being cognizant of one's spoken and written language, you need to be aware of your zones of proximity (Vygotsky, 1978) and the types of interactions you have with all kinds of children. Some teachers seem to be more comfortable when interacting with students whom they perceive to be more like them. Their comfort may be based on race, ethnicity, gender, social class, religion, language, ability, size, or other characteristics. We encourage you to be conscious of your interactions, so you develop positive relationships with all children, with those both like and unlike yourselves.

It may be helpful to invite a colleague into your classroom to watch your interaction styles and to give you some honest feedback. You may not be aware of your patterns, such as where you have placed various kinds of students, where you stand or walk when teaching the class, whom you call upon to answer questions, whether you typically ask certain students difficult or easy questions, and the kinds of feedback and reinforcement you provide to various students following their responses. New teachers are encouraged to ask a mentor in whom they have trust to observe them teaching at different times throughout the day and week. The earlier in one's career a teacher becomes cognizant of interactions, the earlier this person can make improvements that benefit everyone.

OBSERVE GROUPING AND DISCIPLINE PATTERNS

Another important equity issue for new teachers involves the patterns related to grouping and discipline. Many elementary schools are organized for students to learn in groups of students with similar abilities. In schools that follow this strategy of tracking, the advanced readers work with students with the same skills using materials that challenge them appropriately. The less proficient and remedial readers do the same. Generally, children who live in homes with more economic opportunities tend to achieve more in school. In the United States, Anglo families tend to offer more economic opportunities; therefore, Anglo children tend to be placed in the more advanced academic groups, are provided more opportunities, and demonstrate greater achievement in school. These grouping patterns begin early during the elementary school years and continue throughout high school (Ansalone & Biafora, 2004).

Frequently, children who are placed in the more or less advanced reading groups or classes also are placed in similarly leveled math groups or classes. In some elementary schools, the entire class is composed of the more proficient or the less proficient students. This grouping pattern is supported by educators who believe that they can address the abilities of their students more accurately by reducing the range of abilities of students in one classroom. These teachers believe that they can focus on particular needs and optimize out-comes through better use of materials and resources (Sadker & Sadker, 2005).

Unfortunately, this approach results in two long-term, detrimental social outcomes. Students tend to be isolated from interacting with all kinds of students, limiting their opportunities to learn from one another, and students tend to stay in these academic tracks throughout their K–12 schooling. Very quickly, students learn that they have been placed in a particular level of education, usually matched by the preparation and experience of the teacher, the amount and richness of the resources, and the academic and social expectations of the students. As the more proficient groups receive additional support and resources, the academic gaps tend to widen, and the opportunities to move from one track to another tend to lessen (Fritzberg, 2001).

Sadly, there appears to be a disproportionate number of students from the less advanced groups or classes (especially students enrolled in special education classes) who receive harsher discipline. Again, you would benefit from looking closely at the criteria used to organize student groups or classes, the cultural characteristics of the children who are placed in various groups or classes, and the rationale for these decisions. Match your approaches to meeting the needs of your students and improving the educational outcomes for their schools (Skiba, Michael, Nardo, & Peterson 2002).

ENCOURAGE ALL CHILDREN TO RESPECT ALL CHILDREN

Your students will make remarks and display behaviors that reflect comments heard from their families, peers, and the media, behaviors and comments that are prejudicial and hateful. Sometimes you will be a witness to these events; other times, the events will be reported to you by other students, teachers, and even families. You must take a stand and intervene appropriately. You cannot allow for stereotyping and prejudice to occur. You must determine if issues should be addressed quietly among the students involved in the incident or if the issues should be addressed with the entire class. You will find yourself implementing both types of interventions (Beaudoin & Taylor, 2004).

"We have a few bullies at our school, and I think teachers should help stop the bullies."

—Rosie, age 11, Grade 5

It is important that you stop your students when they are speaking or acting hatefully. Listen calmly as they explain their words and actions; redirect their hate to care.

STRIVE FOR EQUITY AND EXCELLENCE FOR ALL CHILDREN

All adults can reflect upon an elementary school teacher who made a significant difference in their lives. That difference may have been related to academic achievement; however, the difference is remembered as being related to social understanding and acceptance. As children, we know we are unique; we know our families are different from some families. The ease we feel in our homes disappears when we step into our classrooms. It is the responsibility of the teacher to mediate the real and/or perceived differences among individuals as they form collaborative communities of learners. Through their words and actions, teachers communicate powerful messages that will stay with a child forever. Teachers need to ensure that every child feels a sense of belonging, a sense of agency, at school.

Another reflection from a new teacher . . .

I had always heard my teachers tell us to take our papers home to parents. When I started teaching, I said the same thing. One day one of my first graders asked me if it was okay to take the paper home to his grandmother. He added that he didn't live with mom or dad right now. Dad was in jail, and mom had gone away. That child's question haunted me; he was coping the best he could and was fortunate to be living with his grandmother. After that day, I became much more attuned to my selection of words. I not only needed to use words that were inclusive of all my students, I needed to let my students know that we live in many different situations and all of them are just fine.

Children come to school bearing the full range of abilities and interests, from all kinds of homes and heritages, and with every type of expectation and reinforcement. Your responsibilities are to accept them for who they are, challenge them to learn all they can in every way you can possibly facilitate, and propel them toward excellence academically, socially, and affectively. Basic to each of these ambitions is the requirement to ensure equity. You must play fair by following democratic principles and guaranteeing social justice, and your fairness must be evident in both formal and informal classroom interactions. Students (and their families) trust their teachers; teachers must maintain that trust. Students are cognizant of the teacher-student interactions in the classroom. They will tell you who the teacher favors, who the "teacher's pets" are.

"One of my teachers didn't always treat all the students the same. She didn't treat the students equally. She didn't show respect for the students. . . . The teacher was always nice to me, but I don't like it when teachers are mean to other students."

—Chris, age 10 ½, Grade 5

Provide all students equal opportunities to obtain information, gain access, and participate fully in the educational process. There is no one right way to teach, learn, or exist in our contemporary schools and society. There is no absolute truth that applies to all people at all times. You will need to learn to trust yourself, find ways to include every student equitably, and be brave in pursuit of these ideals.

MAKE CERTAIN EVERYONE FEELS SAFE AND WELCOME . . .

Every child, every family, and every teacher should feel safe and welcome around the school and in the classroom. Students and their families should feel assured that every child will be treated respectfully and responsibly by the teachers and all other students, so as to optimize outcomes and achievement. You can and will make all the difference in a child's world.

Suggested Activities

1. Think about and discuss how teachers show they care for and are concerned about all their students.

2. Share examples of how teachers incorporate the multicultural perspective in their teaching.

3. Role play how you would handle a classroom situation in which students are behaving in disrespectful ways.

4. Analyze how you speak to and interact with your students. Do you stand as close to the boys as you do the girls? Do you move around the room in a predictable path stopping by the same students more often or for longer than you stop by other students? Do you detect a pattern that correlates to students' ethnicities, heritages, socioeconomic status, or other characteristic?

CHAPTER NINE

Using Instructional Technology

Where are you on the continuum of using instructional technology?

One new teacher revealed . . .

> Technology overwhelms me. There is so much to know, and so much I should be doing with my fourth graders. I'm not sure how to use technology and still cover everything I am supposed to teach!

Another new teacher reports . . .

> Publisher, PowerPoint, Photoshop—those are my three Power Programs. My students love to use these software programs. And, we all use Microsoft Word, Excel, and Kidspiration. I integrate technology as often as possible.

There are numerous forms of technology found in today's classrooms, and it is important that the word "technology" is not used exclusively to mean "computer." Examples of what is referred to as instructional technology also include multimedia such as whiteboards, televisions, VCR players, DVD players, CD players, tape recorders, cameras, overhead projectors, AlphaSmarts, projector systems, printers, scanners, smart boards, and software programs, along with the Internet and e-mail. In addition, a range of assistive technologies are used to support students with special needs, such as voice recognition computer programs. Most school districts are working diligently to develop strategic plans for the acquisition and implementation of technology, and they revise these plans on a regular basis.

We encourage you to view and use technology with your students in the three ways described below: content, processes, and context. Note that these three areas parallel the three aspects of curriculum described in Chapter 5.

Viewing Technology in the Classroom

1. *Content* to be learned, i.e., inventions or tools, with structures and functions, that have been created and continue to change over time;

2. *Processes* to be learned and applied to knowledge acquisition and construction, critical thinking, decision making, and problem solving; and

3. *Contexts* that utilize both the inventions and tools *as well as the technological thinking* in unlimited ways to organize, present, and facilitate data and to help learners move from abstract ideas to concrete products.

UNDERSTAND THE CONTENT OF TECHNOLOGY

The first way to view technology is as content knowledge and information to be learned, constructed, and advanced. The history of the world includes an abundance of technology, inventions, and tools that have been created and modified over time. All of these have dramatically changed the ways we think, act, and believe. The wheel, the printing press, gas-powered machinery, and atomic energy identify just a few of the significant forms of technology that were invented in the past and continue to impact all people's lives today. Learning about how these technological innovations developed over time is fundamental for every elementary school student.

A keen insight is that technology content can be woven easily into daily lessons in literacy, math, science, social studies, and the fine arts, as well as integrated through interdisciplinary units of learning (Roberts & Kellough, 2003). Students benefit greatly from opportunities to explore and discover what was invented, when various forms of technology were invented, and where they were invented. Students want to know how technologies were invented, why they were invented, and who invented them. Students are curious to unearth what obstacles were encountered along the way, who received recognition and credit for the invention and who did not, and how inventions affected society at that time and still affect it today. Every invention is accompanied by a powerful story that can both inform and inspire young learners.

APPLY THE PROCESSES OF TECHNOLOGY

The second way to view technology is as processes and skills applied to critical thinking, decision making, and problem solving—elements of constructivist learning. Such an understanding of and approach toward technology may be a little more challenging for you to comprehend quickly, as most teachers either have not considered this important aspect of technology or simply take technological thinking for granted (presuming it is simply the way we operate in today's world). The vast majority of us were raised with televisions, telephones, cameras, microwave ovens, and computers that have evolved dramatically during our lifetimes. In most cases, we can't even imagine a time without these various forms of technology for daily functions as well as entertainment and educational purposes. We certainly notice differences when technological innovations that we tend to use regularly and expect to be present in our everyday lives are not in use or are inaccessible. How exasperating to figure out directions on a map when MapQuest or Yahoo! Driving Directions is not available!

The acquisition of technology processes and skills empowers us to think and act technologically, and we rely upon this foundation to help us solve problems and construct new knowledge. We begin to look at situations not just as what they are but as what they can be, or we see not just what things can do but what else they could be or do. Gradually, thinking technologically moves from the concrete to the abstract and back to the concrete. Technological thinking patterns have been displayed by many inventors throughout time, as their thoughts and actions enhanced our well-being, increased productivity, and advanced societies.

From a new teacher . . .

> I realized immediately that my sixth-grade students understood and used more technology than I did. This was my chance to let them be the teachers (so everyone could learn from one another). We began a project of designing our own countries. It was amazing to see what my students included as part of their populations' communication systems as well as how my students drew their designs using technology. I asked the students to keep a journal recording their thinking processes. Here's where I discovered their complex thinking patterns moving between abstract and concrete ideas.

APPRECIATE THE CONTEXT OF TECHNOLOGY

The third view of technology combines the physical tools with the academic knowledge and information related to the tools with the technological thinking processes and skills that empower us to create and express ourselves through multiple sources. To fully understand the context of technology, we must recognize both the roles and responsibilities of dispositions and opportunities. Our dispositions or outlooks allow us to see situations in the broadest sense and to approach new challenges optimistically as welcomed opportunities and steps toward meaningful outcomes. We find ourselves asking questions that seek to know not just what something is or what it does but also what else the item could be or do. We view change as both a challenge and a choice to make improvements that could benefit everyone.

When we consider critical thinking, decision making, and problem solving, we realize that both teachers and learners must be equipped fully with the technological knowledge and information as well as the processes and skills to function proficiently and to express themselves productively. Teachers and learners need to be aware of what technology is available, how the technology works independently or in combination with other forms of technology, and how these forms and functions fit for a particular individual or group within a particular space and time.

For example, if fourth-grade students need to develop presentations about specific historical places for their state social studies unit of learning, students could search the Internet for a list of important state historical sites. This procedure would require them to know about the Internet and printers and to be able to use the Internet safely and wisely, to read, and to print documents from the computer. Students would need to know about word processing and printing. Likewise, students would need to know about finding books in the library (through a computer program) and using scanners. Then they would need to know how to use the library computer program and how to scan photographs from books, magazines, newspapers, and brochures.

Students might want to travel to specific locations (thus requiring more technology in the form of transportation) to take digital photographs. Therefore, they would need to know how to use a digital camera and how to insert photographs into their presentation. Finally, the students would need to know about PowerPoint or other slide presentation programs and projector systems. Then the students would need to know how to use each of these tools and how to think technologically, so they could combine their acquired and constructed knowledge to express themselves creatively to their selected audience. Table 9.1 lists technology tools, skills, and resources for a sample historical places project.

Students would also need to know how to behave independently or in a cooperative learning group, delegate tasks, and manage resources, time, and materials. Obviously, the context combines purpose, process, and product into a holistic experience that is both acted upon individually and shared between teacher and learner.

The context of technology determines students' roles as both consumers and producers of technology. Students use technology to produce outcomes that are both high tech and non–high tech. For

Table 9.1   Example of Using Technology for Historical Places Project

Technology-related Tools	Technology-related Skills	Resources
Multimedia computer with Internet access	Access reliable Internet	Books
	Access library program	Articles
Printer	Word processing	Newspapers
Scanner	Print	CDs
Digital camera	Create PowerPoint	Historical sites
PowerPoint software	Insert pictures into PowerPoint	People
		Internet

example, we use digital cameras to take photos that we combine with scanned photos to create illustrated presentations. As we use the technology, we may also discover ways to produce technology by combining various tools. We want our students to see themselves in both perspectives—as consumers of current technology and creators of new technology.

TAKE A TECHNOLOGY INVENTORY

Understanding these purposes of technology will strengthen and prepare you for your classrooms and students. The next step is to take inventory of the available equipment and resources. Frequently, today's classrooms have at least one computer (though it may not be a new one), a monitor, a television, a video or DVD player, tape recorders and headphones, and CD players available or assigned to each classroom. When equipment is housed in your classroom, you can use it with great freedom whenever you need it for teaching and learning. You can display an overhead transparency, show a video, or play a recording as the learning experience develops. You can use the instructional technology with the whole class at once, with small groups of learners, in self-directed centers, or as an individual learning system. You can elect to use multiple forms of technology simultaneously!

Whenever you use instructional technology, practice first and have a back-up plan, in case something fails when you go to use it. It may be something as simple as a bulb burning out or as complicated as the server being "down." Check to see that you have adequate monitors, screens, cables, electrical cords; that the electrical cords are placed safely behind furniture or covered adequately if the cords run across the floor; and that the electrical system can support many pieces of equipment operating at the same time. Also, find out if students are allowed to move and/or operate the technology without your immediate supervision.

Sometimes equipment is shared between two teachers or among a grade level team of teachers. In this case, you will have to coordinate scheduling of equipment, make thoughtful arrangements in advance allowing for the movement of the technology or the students, and maintain the schedule so teachers and students alike can achieve their goals. You may have to change the time at which you teach a subject in order to incorporate particular forms of technology, or you may want to team-teach with another teacher to maneuver more resourcefully.

Another common way that school personnel have organized technology is to house most of it in one central location, such as the library, media center, or computer lab. Generally, in these situations, equipment can be checked out to teachers to use in their classrooms for a specified length of time, such as two weeks. Again, you must plan your learning experiences to coordinate with your academic and technological outcomes.

In some schools, teachers take their students to a lab at set or arranged times to use equipment. For example, the newest computers may be in one room with a computer teacher; students are taken to the lab for 30–60 minutes each week for structured instruction. The computer teacher introduces skills such as navigating, game playing, and keyboarding. Frequently, the computer teacher collaborates with the classroom teacher, so the computer lab time is used to fulfill classroom assignments at the same time. It is helpful to review the instructional technology standards (see below) and expectations for elementary students. You can collaborate as to how best to integrate the technology standards across your curriculum, instruction, and assessment.

As your personal technological proficiency increases and your experience with applications advances, you will likely be in a position to request additional tools. Identify what resources you would like to have and what level, if any, of training you and your students will need; by doing this, you will be prepared with a "wish list" when funding and professional development opportunities become available.

GET TO KNOW TECHNOLOGY STANDARDS

Members of the International Society for Technology in Education (ISTE) have written standards and benchmarks within each standard that identify educational goals related to the three purposes of instructional technology: content, processes, and context. The standards specify what students should know, do, and believe in PreK–12 to be technology literate. They cover becoming proficient; understanding ethical and other issues; and using tools to record information, produce work, communicate with others, conduct research, solve problems, and make decisions.

The technology standards promote critical thinking, thoughtful conversations, and creative strategies among teachers. These standards explore a variety of approaches for teaching technology and integrating it throughout the grade level curriculum, instruction, and assessment, with applications in all subject areas and all models of teaching (Joyce & Weil, 2003). Benchmarks of performance indicators have been written as a general set of profiles for students in grades PreK–2, 3–5, 6–8, and 9–12 to promote a smooth and steady development of knowledge, skills, and dispositions throughout school. You can plan, facilitate, and assess learning *about* technology (content), learning *with* technology (processes), and learning *through* technology (context) to ensure comprehension, productivity, decision making, and lifelong learning.

The technology standards also promote equity. Not every child brings the same background experiences with technology literacy from home; not every child will exhibit the same skills or be able to interact equally with the instructional technology at school. Not every child will exhibit the same levels of achievement and excitement about using multimedia. The National Council for Accreditation of Teacher Education (NCATE), endorsed by ISTE, provides four guidelines to ensure information, access, and opportunity for all students:

1. Demonstrate awareness of resources for adaptive assistive devices for students with special needs;

2. Demonstrate knowledge of equity, ethics, legal, and human issues concerning use of computers and technology;

3. Design, deliver, and assess student learning activities that integrate computers/technology for a variety of student grouping strategies and for diverse student populations; and

4. Design student learning activities that foster equitable, ethical, and legal use of technology by students.

PLAN YOUR USES OF INSTRUCTIONAL TECHNOLOGY

Now that you are well grounded and aware of your resources, it is time to start designing the uses of instructional technology in your classroom. Be creative and open to the ideas of your students. You can integrate technology easily in many different ways (Wentworth, Earle, & Connell, 2004).

"I like to read stories and put on little shows . . . We get to write our own scripts. Sometimes we write them on the computers. I like computers."

—Trevor, age 9, Grade 3

Use of technology in the classroom varies depending on time, space, equipment, abilities of students, and abilities of teachers. You can integrate one or more of these approaches every day in your classroom:

Demonstration Station for Whole Group Instruction—the instructional technology, e.g., overhead projector, television screen, computer monitor, is placed where all the students can see the display easily (usually in the center of the classroom). The teacher guides the students through the displayed content or applicable processes. Students may participate firsthand in the experiential learning by posing inquiries, guiding the operations, recording data, and analyzing outcomes.

Cooperative Group Station—instructional technology, e.g., computer, tape recorder, video player, is located to one side or in a corner of the classroom where a small group of students can gather easily. Groups may be working on the same or different parts of the same unit of learning and will share results with one another. Time is given during the day for working at the station, so the teacher can assist each group.

Learning Centers—multiple forms of instructional technology are located to the sides or in the corners of the classroom where one to three students can work independently or as a small group. Assignments at the learning centers can be related to the units of learning directly or indirectly. All students can go to a learning center at once at your direction, or the students may go to their assigned centers when they have completed other tasks.

Independent Research/Communication Stations—multiple forms of instructional technology are located to the sides or in the corners of the classroom where one to three students can work as they desire. Sign-up sheets will ensure equitable access and use. Factors to consider include length of time at stations, supplies needed, and measurements of productivity.

From a new teacher . . .

> I have only one computer in my classroom, so at least once a day we gather around it where everyone can see the operations and the screen. I guide a different student in conducting the searches or recording the data. For reading, we look up titles nominated for the state award and keep a running record describing the books we have read. For math, we search for information related to problem solving such as the cost of an item years ago and maintain a table of interesting items. For science, we research information about various parts of the United States and draw a map recording our findings. For social studies, we look for laws and note how people react to changes on a time line. I want my students to know how to get on and off the computer quickly and how to use it as another valuable resource.

IDENTIFY LEARNING OUTCOMES

It is essential to coordinate your approach with your expectations. Listed below are four outcomes for using instructional technology, especially computers, to increase media literacy.

Short-term Technical Skill Building—Students are introduced to a particular form of instructional technology to learn why, how, and when to use it appropriately, e.g., computer software program, word processing, and so forth, and to increase their acquisition and construction of knowledge. This is most effective when all students can practice simultaneously and demonstrate their proficiency for the teacher immediately.

Small Group Instruction—This approach is much like short-term technical skill building only the teacher works with a small group requiring specific instruction. The rest of the class is engaged in other learning activities.

Review and Practice—Students work at independent stations to accomplish specific outcomes for reviewing and practicing prior learning. Access may be incorporated into the school day at allocated time or as reinforcement for completing other tasks.

Communication—Students work individually at computers to communicate with e-pals through Internet chat rooms and e-mail. Students can exchange ideas with experts, peers, and their teachers.

GUIDE STUDENTS IN GAINING INFORMATION

The Internet empowers students to gain information from a variety of sources. It enables students to participate in conversations with other students through e-mail and chat rooms. Teachers should supervise students' activities closely. Place computer monitors in an area where activities can be viewed without obstruction. Interact with students as they plan and conduct their searches; discuss the sites they wish to explore, the people with whom they want to chat, and, later on, the resources they consulted and the information they have found.

When you conduct a search on the Internet, we recommend that you use a popular search engine. Look for Web sites from well-known and reputable organizations and agencies. An effective Web site shows the most important information on its home page, and the home page can be viewed clearly and in its entirety on the computer monitor. Such sites are colorful yet not distracting; usually, they include photographs of people and products with large and easy-to-read print. The links, displayed with icons and words, should also be easy to understand and use.

Beware that not all of the information found on the Internet is accurate or comes from authentic sources. Conducting a search on the Internet may generate sites that are not appropriate for your students. You or your school may want to install filtering software that prevents your students from accessing inappropriate sites. As the teacher, you will want to establish an acceptable use policy (AUP). Many districts and schools have such policies in place as well.

Elementary students should be guided toward never using rude or mean language in an e-mail or chat room and not sharing their passwords with other students. They need to be reminded not to share personal information, send a picture or video, provide credit card information, or arrange a face-to-face meeting. Students should be advised that if someone on a Web site or in a chat room offers gifts, money, or "something for nothing," they should tell the teacher immediately and show the teacher the site. This also applies if any information found on a Web site makes a student feel uncomfortable or confused. Franek (2005) encourages teachers to address the issue of *cyberbullying* and to create procedures for students to follow if they feel victimized.

It will be easy for students to spend a great amount of time "searching the Web." This type of exploration will be beneficial, and you can allow students some time for searching. However, most teachers identify a select variety of Web sites from which students can choose to do research. Your narrowing the search will economize on time yet offer choices for students. Plus it will ensure that they use appropriate sources.

EXPRESS LEARNING TECHNOLOGICALLY

When using technology to gain information, student authorship increases dramatically. Students like writing and drawing on computers. They enjoy completing Web quests, concept maps, time lines, databases, and spreadsheets. As students learn to organize their own research projects, they not only gain information through instructional technologies, they record and evaluate the collected data. This last step increases higher order and critical thinking, decision making, and problem solving, as students become more analytical and selective not only in their acquisition of data but also in their recording processes. These accomplishments transfer readily to new learning situations.

By working cooperatively, students teach one another and propel their learning beyond most teachers' expectations as they learn to think technologically. Students can brainstorm and organize ideas using various forms of software to create concept maps. They hone their skills for asking questions, taking notes, and synthesizing information. Students also can engage in thought-provoking inquiry as they examine topics and issues from multiple perspectives. These processes and skills are paramount for completing both single and complex assignments such as those involved in project-based learning.

The final step that completes the sequence of gaining and recording data focuses on students' abilities to express their learning. Outcomes can be expressed through overhead transparencies, PowerPoint or other slide program demonstrations, brochures, or video and interactive discussions. The ideas are limited only by the imagination.

You will want to design your curriculum, instruction, and assessment to match the learning needs and wants of your students as well as your own knowledge and skills. You must be aware of your students' abilities and interests. Take time to facilitate and balance your expectations for technology with other academic expectations. As you consider your calendar, develop a plan for introducing skills and technology throughout the year.

BEWARE OF THE DIGITAL DIVIDE

Although the number of PreK–12 schools and classrooms across the United States with multiple forms of technology, especially computers, has risen dramatically over the last five years, that does not mean that all schools and all classrooms are equipped with the same resources (Rother, 2005). The varying rates of availability communicate a strong message of possibilities and potential to you, your students, and their families. Likewise, possibilities and potential are limited in schools and classrooms where technology is available but either personnel is not hired to guide students and assist you or teachers choose not to use the technology fully.

Schools across the United States are not funded equitably due to the structure of individual states' school funding formulas. Budgets are used to provide the most immediate and necessary items, which do not always include instructional technology. And, far too often, these schools are inner city or rural schools providing educational services for the neediest of our nation's children. These children are being raised in homes where technology is not a regular part of daily living, and parents are not likely to provide instructional technology, such as a computer, or take their children to a library or community recreation center after school where these resources may be available.

Overwhelmingly, teachers continue to see that children from homes with higher socioeconomic levels of income and advanced levels of education, and particularly Anglo boys, tend to be more interested, supported, and proficient in their competence and confidence with instructional technology (Morse, 2004). These trends grow stronger as boys progress through middle school and high school. Fewer girls and minorities of either gender seek the high school Advanced Placement classes, university degrees, or professional careers in engineering and computer-related fields. Students with special learning needs, such as English language learners and special education, students, are not provided as much access or as many opportunities with instructional technology as other students. New teachers need to be aware of these trends as they plan and facilitate learning experiences featuring instructional technology in their classrooms to ensure equity for all.

INCREASE YOUR ADMINISTRATIVE EFFICIENCY

Computer technology provides helpful administrative tools for recording attendance, monitoring progress, following IEPs, and grading. Many schools use software programs to house student achievement data. Data on individual students is then readily available to guide instruction. Other software tools assist with planning curriculum, developing daily lesson plans, and mapping long-range curriculum outcomes. You can use technology to prepare parent communications and newsletters (written by you alone or by you with your students). Through e-mail, you can facilitate communication with mentors and colleagues, plan meetings, and exchange information. Teachers are relying more and more on technology to achieve their goals.

ADVANCE YOUR KNOWLEDGE AND ABILITIES

As you walk around the school, look for others who are willing to share what they have learned. Check with your district and county office of education to see what types of professional development are held. There may be convenient summer workshops or afterschool training. Some districts now provide online, on-demand training! Consider classes, such as PowerPoint and Photoshop, offered by local parks and recreation centers, community colleges, or the local university.

LET TECHNOLOGY BE YOUR FRIEND . . .

Technology will always be essential to both educational environments and teaching/learning experiences. You are encouraged to welcome all forms of technology into your repertoire and enjoy everything that technology has to offer. Think of it in the adage that technology is both the means and the end. In your classroom, you can teach *about* technology as *content,* teach *with* technology as a *process,* and teach *through* technology as a *context.* In your professional development, you can use technology for information gathering, data recording, and word processing, as part of your classroom preparation, grade analysis, student communications, university studies, and career advancement. The secret is to let technology work for you.

Suggested Activities

1. Develop a pre-assessment for students to determine their computer technology proficiency.

2. Observe how other teachers address the four outcomes for using instructional technology, and evaluate the student responses.

3. Interview students on the role of technology in their lives and what their goals are for the future.

4. Begin a collection of Web sites for science and social studies topics.

CHAPTER TEN

Developing as a Professional

Teaching is a performance profession, not unlike that of acting on a stage. Our audiences study our costumes, words, and actions; they decide, based on these appearances, whether we are convincing in our roles or whether we are even worth noticing. Parents, colleagues, and staff, as well, form strong impressions of our skills and levels of professional competence based on the ways we present ourselves. In the beginning of the school year, it is particularly important to establish yourself as a person worthy of respect. You will want to create a professional image (Cattani, 2002).

Your clothes tell a story about you, especially to impressionable youth whose identities are so tied up in their clothing. You would only have to go back into your own memories to recall teachers who wore strange shoes, or out-of-style clothing, or inappropriate outfits to realize just how important it is to dress for success as a teacher.

Likewise, your colleagues will be curious to talk with you. What you say or repeat about people will quickly reveal the type of professional you are. Your interactions with colleagues will take place primarily before and after school or during lunch at both formal and informal gatherings. Ironically, your professional image may be determined by your colleagues during the time when you perceive you can relax the most. Be aware of your presence during lunch and planning periods. We want you to develop successfully as a professional, and this chapter is filled with all kinds of valuable ideas to help you achieve this success.

DRESS FOR SUCCESS

Most elementary school teachers wear clothing that is comfortable and contemporary. Elementary school teachers are moving around all the time. Teachers need to make sure they can sit comfortably in adult-sized chairs, children-sized chairs, or even on the floor. Teachers may find themselves bending over or getting down on their knees frequently. They will handle paint, glue, crayons, markers and other art supplies. Dress for the many activities you'll be involved in during the day.

Women will be comfortable wearing suits, dresses, skirts with sweaters, skirts and blouses, and dress pants with suit jackets, blouses, or sweaters. Men will feel comfortable wearing suits, slacks and sports coats, and dress pants with collared or button-down shirts (adding sweaters when it is cold). Dress in layers that you can put on and take off easily as you move throughout the day and around the building. And all teachers need to wear comfortable shoes.

Some teachers will have alternative dress codes because of what they teach. For example, PE teachers usually wear shorts and collared shirts, often with the school emblem. But this type of dress may be restricted to the gyms and the fields. Art teachers may wear large shirts or smocks to protect their clothing. Usually, the large shirts or smocks are worn over their regular teacher-type clothing.

You also want your clothing to provide adequate coverage. Today's fashions for young adults may expose more skin or be more form fitting than is appropriate for classrooms. Try on your clothing, stand in front of a large mirror, and pretend you are teaching as you would normally teach. Watch to see that your clothing covers you adequately and lets you move as you want. If you have any hesitations or doubts about an outfit, save it for the weekends. We strongly encourage you to be aware of how your colleagues dress, to know how your principal expects you to dress, to read the faculty handbook for policies regarding professional dress, and to make wise choices for yourself.

In particular, know if and when you are allowed to wear jeans and the kind of jeans you may wear to work. Some schools allow their teachers to dress more casually on Fridays. Many schools encourage their teachers to wear the school colors or clothing with jeans on Fridays. You will want to listen to your principal, ask your colleagues, and follow their pattern. You may want to invest in a school shirt early in your career.

Use Clothing as a Teaching Tool

You may want to purchase a lab coat or similar kind of jacket to wear in the classroom. This type of coat or jacket will protect your clothing from chalk, chalk dust, markers, glue, paint, and other materials you use throughout the day. A coat or jacket with large pockets allows you to keep supplies, such as keys, pencils, pens, paper, markers, scissors, and maybe even a playground whistle, in your pockets while you move around the classroom helping students individually and in small groups. Some teachers like to wear an apron or a cloth tool belt with pockets to achieve the same outcome.

And clothing can also be used to emphasize points you wish to make in teaching. For social studies, you may wear a kimono when introducing an integrated unit of learning about Japan. An art teacher might wear a shirt with an impressionist painting on the front. To introduce a math lesson, you could wear a shirt with a geometric pattern. Even more inventive, a teacher may dress up in period costume to attract student interest in a social studies unit on a particular era (Gallavan, 2003).

From a first-year teacher . . .

> I wanted to tell my students all about the upcoming winter Olympics, but I wanted to do this in a way that would capture their attention. I pretended that we were having a guest speaker and wrote the guest speaker's name on the board. Then I went into the hallway to get the guest speaker. Quickly I put on an exercise jump suit over my regular teacher-looking clothing. I re-entered the classroom using a different voice announcing that I was the guest speaker. I asked where the teacher was and looked down on the speaker's table. There was a note from the teacher explaining that the teacher had been called away, how excited the students were about the guest speaker's visit, and how good they were.
>
> The students knew I was playing the part of the guest speaker, but no one said a word. I leaped right into my talk illustrated with maps and all kinds of artifacts. The students were spellbound with my presentation and the information. When I had finished my role-playing, I explained that it was time for me to leave and that I would look for their teacher as I left the building. Then, when I was back in the hallway, I removed my outer jumpsuit and came back into the classroom. I asked the students if they had seen our guest speaker and to tell me what they had learned. The students couldn't wait to share everything. I was amazed how much fun this was.

TUNE IN TO THE WEATHER

Your wardrobe selections will depend directly on your weather. Some of you will be teaching in colder climates; some of you will be teaching in warmer climates or wetter climates or quite sunny climates. We strongly encourage you to select an all-purpose sweater or jacket that you can keep in your personal closet at school. Buy a durable pair of sunglasses and maybe a hat, and keep them at school. Since you will be going outdoors frequently, you want to protect your eyes from the sun and wind. You may want to buy an eyeglass leash so you can keep your sunglasses around your neck, especially if you join in the sports and games on the playground. (You probably have a playground whistle on a leash, too, so you can keep these together in the top drawer of your desk or on a hook close to the classroom door.)

You want to be prepared with a raincoat and an oversized umbrella for rainy days. If you are teaching where there is harsher weather, you will want to store warm gloves, a scarf, and winter boots at school. Because bus and recess duties mean they will be outside regularly, many elementary school teachers purchase a durable, all-purpose or recess coat, so they are prepared for every kind of weather.

REMEMBER YOU ARE A ROLE MODEL

Although we have mentioned this in other chapters, we want to re-emphasize that you are a role model when it comes to your appearance. Your students will notice what you wear and what you don't wear. They will talk about you and imitate you. This applies not only to your clothing but also to your professional interactions and personal habits too. You know you need to be fully aware of where you stand in the classroom, where you walk as you move around the classroom, and how you approach students. It is natural to feel more comfortable with some of your students. You want to be sure that you are providing the same amount of attention and help to each of your students. Likewise, you want to decide whether to hug your students or give them "high fives" and so forth, and, if you do engage in these informal interactions, you want to interact equally and appropriately with all your students. Again, you want to treat your students equitably.

You also want to be aware of your mannerisms, such as creating facial expressions, playing with your hair, blowing your nose, scratching, and so on. Your students will imitate you quickly. Don't be surprised if you begin hearing your students using your favorite expressions. Changing your interactions and expressions can modify your students words and actions easily . . . without any direct guidance from you at all.

KNOW YOUR COMMUNITY

It is helpful to know the people in your community. You may be teaching in a more formal school, a less formal school, or a special school with very different kinds of expectations. Therefore, you need to know the kinds of students, their families, and the neighborhood quite well as you plan your wardrobe and attend to your appearance.

Trust us: the students and their families will talk about you. In addition to your wardrobe and appearance, they will know your vehicle.

This also means they will know exactly when you are and when you are not at school. Some teachers drive fancy or sporty cars. It can be rather awkward if you are a new young teacher just out of college and driving an expensive vehicle. Although it is none of the students' and their families' business, what you drive and what they presume about you will become their conversation starters. Sadly, you may want to wait awhile to buy that new car or trade vehicles with your spouse during your first year of teaching. Also, you probably want to make sure the inside of your car is clean. Someone will be looking into it sooner than you expect.

Some communities also want to know about your family. Teachers are just like all other people and live in many different configurations. Some of today's teachers are married; some share their lives with a significant other. The significant other may be of the opposite or the same gender. You may or may not have children. You will have to decide if, how, and when to introduce the people in your life to your students and their families. Likewise, you may be ending a relationship or a marriage. You do not need to share all the parts of your life with your students, their families, or your colleagues; however, it is helpful to have a response ready for when they inquire. We believe that elementary school students view their teachers as part of their own families. Most likely, you will be asking all kinds of questions about their families and encouraging them to share through discussion and writing. Please know that your students will follow your lead and ask you the same kinds of questions. Be sensitive to protect your family and your students' families.

Women elementary school teachers tend to be called Mrs. regardless of their marital status. Students and their families just seem to defer to Mrs. first. If you are an unmarried woman, you may call yourself Miss or Ms. Tell your students and their families when you meet them what you want to be called. You probably want to select and establish your title as soon as you accept your position. The school will be publishing your name in many places. They may have nameplates or business cards prepared for you too.

SELECT YOUR WORDS AND ACTIONS MINDFULLY

Just as your appearance is important for comfort and success, so are your words and actions. You will spend most of your out-of-the-classroom time planning with colleagues, attending meetings, or eating lunch in the faculty lounge. Although these seem like times and places to relax and refresh for the classroom, they also are the times and places when and where you should maintain a professional presence. Too often, teachers spend time out of their classrooms discussing their students, their students' parents, or even their colleagues in the building in ways that might not be considered polite or professional.

It is essential that you listen carefully and select your words and actions mindfully. Your remarks may begin to paint a certain type of image or reputation about you that you do not intend to create. Likewise, you may not fully understand or appreciate someone else's words or actions.

Be just as aware of your interactions when you are outside of the class as you are when you are teaching. Your goal is to accept and respect others in ways that are fair and consistent. You want to be taken seriously, yet you want to balance your care and concern with playfulness and humor. You want to aspire to these goals with your colleagues as well as your students and their families. You have much to learn during planning periods, meetings, and lunch. Take advantage of these opportunities to hone your professionalism. We provide you with some tips to help you along the way.

CONSIDER VARIOUS LUNCH LOCATIONS

Check out the faculty lounge early in the school year. You want to know who eats lunch there, especially if most of the teachers in your grade level share this time and space on a regular basis. Because lunch periods overlap, teachers and teaching assistants from other grade levels will be finishing their lunches as you arrive. And most likely, the specials teachers from art, music, and PE eat in the lounge, so lunch is a good time for you to visit with other teachers from other grade levels and areas of specialization. Eating in the lounge is viewed both positively and negatively. This can be a place for great socialization. People get to know one another personally as well as professionally.

However, the lounge can become quite chatty, and the conversations may make you uncomfortable. Sometimes, when teachers share over lunch, they forget to maintain professionalism. They may express a strong opinion about a national concern, a school policy, or a principal's decision. They may spread gossip by repeating a story that has no validity or value. Gossip is particularly unsavory when the story pertains to school personnel, the students, or their families.

We have known teachers who have eaten in the lounge simply to hear the gossip that they could repeat later. These teachers are no more professional than the teachers who originated the story. Be aware of what you hear and what you say, both in and out of the lounge. That pertains to talking off campus too. Teachers tend to talk about school regardless of their location. You hear them in restaurants and at coffee shops. Professionalism demands that you always keep confidential information to yourself and that you consider what you say about work, how you say it, and who might overhear you.

Some teachers do not eat lunch in the lounge. They prefer either to work independently in their own classrooms or to eat with a few selected teachers—their own grade level team of teachers or special friends throughout the building. As must be readily apparent, teachers group themselves together during lunch according to a number of variables: the geographic proximity of their rooms, their ages (older and younger), their political opinions or lifestyles, their interests, their teaching specialties, or their physical or social attractiveness, to mention just a few. You will find it fascinating research just to observe the various groups in action and to try to figure out what binds them together.

You might want to try all the available lunchtime options during the first few weeks of school, so you know who eats lunch where and with whom. Most likely, you'll be attracted to eating with your grade level teachers either in one teacher's classroom, your shared planning space, or the lounge. These teachers follow the same schedule as you and teach the same kinds of students. You have much in common with these teachers and will benefit from forming a cohesive team.

From time to time, you may enjoy eating lunch with the students. Visit the lunchroom. Sit down with a group. Or invite them to bring their lunches to your room. You'll have a chance to talk to them informally. Let them lead the conversation. Let them ask you questions. Learn about their worlds by listening rather than controlling the conversation. Sometimes, they might even forget you are a teacher, or even an adult, and a whole new world will open up before your eyes and ears in which you will truly get a feeling for what it's like to be a child again.

CULTIVATE YOUR ASSOCIATIONS WISELY

Many teachers begin eating with the same group of teachers and never change their patterns. They tend to keep the same routine every day, perhaps for years, and never get to know other teachers or teaching assistants located throughout the school. You may be viewed as standoffish or hard to know if you eat by yourself or with the same few colleagues every day. Try to break your routine so you get to know more people.

Regardless of the place you choose, consider carefully the consequences of your decision. Some groups are notorious for complaining and whining. It can be very depressing to hear adults berate the students and their parents day in and day out. Some people can be quite cynical about the state of education and the teaching profession. Every lunch period is spent taking turns describing how awful things are in the school, how unmotivated and unruly the kids are today, and how nonsupportive the administration is. Then, particular staff members are selected as a focus for bash and gossip. Even if some of the complaints and criticisms are true, a new teacher does not need to be subjected to such negative energy in the middle of the day. Furthermore, such teachers will not want to have someone like you around who is upbeat and enthusiastic; their atmosphere thrives on pessimism.

In other lunch groups, strategic planning takes place. Teachers plan a field trip, an assembly, or an interdisciplinary unit. They brainstorm new ideas, share techniques that work, and take pride in their successes. They exchange ideas on classroom management and discipline or even compare notes about what works with some students who are particularly tough to handle. These are high-energy, motivated teachers who keep students' best interests in mind. Such teachers will welcome a new addition; their atmosphere thrives on optimism.

Some lunch groups develop a norm in which any school-related conversation is prohibited. These teachers prefer to talk instead about their personal lives, their families and friends, social and political events, books and movies, or community activities. Such individuals prefer to get away from school for a little while; they want to get to know one another, not as teachers but as human beings.

Every school will have its own options available, centered not only on larger groups but also on smaller arrangements of two and three teachers who get together. As much as you will feel the attraction to settle down by yourself or with another new teacher you have befriended, force yourself to reach out to others. Even if you later decide you'd rather eat alone or with one friend, you will at least have circulated enough within the school to meet the faculty and staff and know what options are available.

Wherever you eat lunch, don't try to grade papers or take care of other paperwork. Many teachers' unions worked very hard to get a "duty free" lunch, and you may be reproached by colleagues, some gently and some not so gently, if you bring papers to work on or even mail to read during lunch.

You must build into your day some structures that will keep you mentally alert and physically nourished. There are few jobs as exhausting as that of an elementary school teacher, and the lunch period provides a critical time for you to replenish your energy, both nutritionally and emotionally, before you once again jump back into the fray. The social and professional support of eating with others is invaluable.

Maintain Confidentialities

As a teacher, you will be told much information that you have to keep confidential. The information may relate to principals, colleagues, students, and their families. You will know about your students' academic progress, health concerns, free and reduced lunch options, and, in some cases, legal records. You will be given forms that you must file in safe places away from your students and possibly their parents who volunteer in or visit your classroom. And you may garner information directly from the students about their families, details that you are obligated to report to the authorities. Various school personnel, such as the special education faculty, nurse, and principals, will inform you annually of the procedures for reporting student information that you must share with authorities.

In general, when you are asked a question or asked to comment on a subject or an individual, if you feel the requested information should remain confidential, stay silent. Treat other people as you would want someone to treat you. Discuss confidential information only when it is relevant and necessary. If you do not know information, do not speculate.

If you are uncomfortable with the conversations going on around you, change the topic of the conversation. You can always talk about an upcoming school event or the weather. If the situation continues, we encourage you to get up and leave the room quietly.

It is important to talk professionally at all times and in all places. This applies both on and off campus. You are not just a teacher from eight to five o'clock and when you are at school. You are a teacher representing a particular school and school district as long as you are their employee.

KEEP AND PREPARE FOR APPOINTMENTS

We cannot overemphasize the importance of making and keeping appointments with your colleagues. This is especially true when meetings involving many different professionals and, perhaps, parents have been scheduled. These actions, similar to the other previously described traits, will define your degree of professionalism. Your students, their parents, and your colleagues all depend on you to plan curriculum, facilitate instruction, conduct assessment, and be accountable for many different aspects of your job.

Take time to be prepared for your appointments. If you are meeting with a parent, review the student's file and progress reports. Collect samples of the student's work to share with the parent. Have copies of the assignments and the assessments available to show the parent. Consider ways that you can improve communication with the student and the parent. Sometimes, it may be appropriate for you to ask a colleague such as the specials teacher, the special education teacher, or the principal to join the conference.

If you are meeting with a colleague about a student, again, bring the appropriate documents and tentative plan of action. If you are meeting with a colleague to plan a program, bring your calendar, planner, faculty handbook, pencil, paper, and other materials that would be helpful during the appointment. Too often, teachers, especially new teachers, simply show up for appointments without preparing for the purpose of the meeting or without the tools necessary to help expedite matters. You want to appear professional; that means you want to show that you have done your homework and are ready to move forward.

Here's a secret for you: keep a pad of paper, notebook, or three-ring binder with a pencil case filled with pens and pencils near your calendar and planning book and handy at all times. This way you will be prepared for planned or unplanned meetings, telephone calls, etc. You never know when you will need to record important information or jot down a valuable idea.

ATTEND TO PERSONAL MATTERS OUTSIDE OF SCHOOL

Even though you are not with students immediately before or after school, during planning time, or at lunchtime, these are not the times to place personal phone calls, except if you need to quickly make some appointments. Generally, there are only a few telephone lines coming into a school. They should be used for educational purposes rather than your personal matters. Even if you are using your own cell telephone, you should not be making personal calls at school; you need to be attending to your job when you are at work.

Also, do not bring your own children to school with you unless it is a special event for families and you are not responsible for your own students. Some teachers' children attend schools that follow different school calendars and may have dismissed classes on days that you are holding classes or have a noninstructional workday. You need to make appropriate arrangements for your children away from school, regardless of what your colleagues think of your children. You cannot give your total attention to either your students or your colleagues and school tasks when you are supervising your own children.

School is not the place for personal projects such as arts and crafts, your children's fundraisers, college homework, personal beauty regimes, and so forth. You probably detect that we have seen all of these behaviors, prompting us to emphasize the importance of dedicating the planning space to schoolwork and keeping your personal life at home. The planning rooms and faculty lounges are shared spaces that need to be respected by everyone.

STRIVE FOR PROFESSIONALISM EVERYWHERE . . .

Becoming a teacher is not just about teaching and learning. Although you will be consumed with developing curriculum, planning instruction, and aligning assessments throughout your career, you also want to be attentive to your appearance and actions both in and out of the classroom. Teachers are professionals. They are trusted to present themselves as individuals who posses large amounts of content knowledge as well as instructional or pedagogical expertise. Teachers must understand and appreciate both the school and the community where they work. They must select their words and actions carefully, so they appear positive and professional at all times.

Your goal is to be a great teacher . . . the best teacher you can be. So now you want to look like a teacher, sound like a teacher, and act like a teacher. Reflect upon the great teachers of your childhood or the ones with whom you have worked as you prepared to become a teacher. We presume that these outstanding role models inspire an image in you that will help carry you through your career.

Suggested Activities

1. As you observe in schools, note how the various teachers, staff, and principals dress throughout the school year. Consider your wardrobe, and see if what you have will be suitable for teaching. If not, plan what you need to acquire.

2. Walk around a school, maybe your own school, during lunch and note all the different places people are eating. Which place(s) seem comfortable to you? In which groups do you find the people supportive and recharging? How will you help create and maintain a positive environment?

3. In the privacy of your home, practice the words to say to colleagues when you want to excuse yourself and leave because your colleagues are being negative. Rehearse ways to change the topic of conversation when it becomes uncomfortable.

4. Make a list of items that you want to pack in your book bag so you are ready for all kinds of weather. Make a second list of items that you want to collect so you are ready for all kinds of meetings and conversations.

Chapter Eleven

Connecting With Students

It is through your relationships with students that you affect and influence them most dramatically (Erickson, 2000). You only have to recall your own most important mentors and effective teachers to realize that it wasn't the information they knew that was so important or how skilled they were in organizing their lessons; rather, it was who they were as human beings. Somehow, some way, they were able to connect with you so that you felt respected and cared for. You weren't just a student to them; you were someone who truly mattered (Fay & Funk, 1998).

The connection that you felt between you and your best teachers was built on trust and caring. These people in your life seemed to be able to reach you at a core level. They nourished not only your mind but also your heart and spirit. During times when you were most impressionable, these teachers were there for you. With them in your corner, you learned that school was safe and learning was fun.

Implement Ongoing Classroom Management

Many different elements of classroom management contribute to success: setting expectations for behavior, controlling the flow of activity, handling discipline problems, and keeping students engaged and motivated to learn (Bevel & Jordan, 2003). It is important to maintain prevention strategies along with intervention strategies to support your students throughout the year.

Prevention. By creating a comfortable environment and establishing a caring rapport with your students, you set the stage for peaceful, cooperative classes. In Chapter 4, we walked you through the procedures for establishing expectations and consequences together. You will also need to communicate rules and enforce them consistently. Routines mentioned in Chapter 7 will help your classroom to function efficiently.

Here are other prevention activities:

- Welcoming your students to the room each day gives you an opportunity to interact with them as they enter and to give them a little individual attention as the day starts.
- Planning for smooth transitions from one activity to the next will help prevent discipline problems.
- Using highly motivational activities for instruction creates attentiveness. When you immediately capture students' interest and make the topic relevant, you will gain their attention at the beginning of the learning experience, and they will have little time to act out.

You should also note (and perhaps recall from your own experiences as a student) that many students are not particularly interested in what is happening in school academically, as they do not find it relevant to their most cherished interests (acceptance, approval, entertainment). They are forced to learn things that they would never select for themselves. They are subjected to classroom routines and procedures that are, at best, boring and, at worst, quite annoying.

> "One teacher would give us directions every five minutes. I just wanted to be left alone and do it myself."
>
> —Keisha, age 9, Grade 3

Sometimes, the learning is simply too hard for students and not developmentally appropriate. No wonder some students act out and become difficult to handle. In a sense, they are honestly communicating what they feel, which is boredom, anger, and frustration. Of course, your job is to engage students while helping them stay within appropriate boundaries (Kottler & Kottler, 2000). Here are some secrets to help you avoid such situations:

- Watch and listen; most students will tell you exactly what they need to be successful.
- Talk with your students as a group and individually when you or they are confused and frustrated.
- Keep your sense of humor, and remember that students want to enjoy school.

Mild Intervention. At times, students will lose interest and begin to daydream or engage in another activity. Minor discipline problems are to be expected. After all, you are working with growing children. If this behavior does not interrupt the class, such as when a student is simply looking out the window, you can respond in several ways. If it is not serious and will probably go away in a minute or two, consider the following options:

- Ignore undesired behavior. If it isn't bothering the other students and won't distract you, wait and see what happens.
- Stand near the student. Sometimes just moving closer will encourage a student to refocus attention to the assigned task.
- Use nonverbal communication, such as pointing to the task, to redirect attention.
- Initiate a verbal response. Gently, speak to the student to gain attention and draw the individual to the task.
- Use an "I" message. Tell the student how you feel when the student is not paying attention.
- Make a direct appeal. Ask the student to refocus on the lesson.
- Remind the student of class rules, expectations, and consequences.
- Try using humor to deal with the situation. Speak with a light and friendly tone in a positive way to bring the distracted individual back to the task at hand.
- Offer assistance if you discover the student is distracted due to an inability to complete the task.

Major Interventions. When discipline becomes an issue, you will have to become more active and direct in your responses. You will need to quickly communicate with the student. Also, you may need to involve other people from outside the classroom. Possible actions include the following:

- Request that the student put away whatever object currently has gained attention.

- Remove the stimulus. Take the object away. If it is not a weapon or something that should be returned directly to a parent, assure the student that you will return the object at the end of the school day.
- Encourage involvement. Privately, talk to the student. Find something that would be attractive or intriguing to him or her. Give the student responsibility for something in the classroom.
- Give a logical consequence. Remind the student of what action will follow if the behavior continues.
- Withdraw a privilege. Let the student know there will be a change in the future, if compliance with the class rules does not take place.
- Change seats. Have the student sit in another location.
- Write a note to the student. In private, communicate your response to the unwanted behavior. You may be able to do this during class, if you are discreet.
- Contact a parent or guardian. Call home and discuss the behavior.
- Send the student to time out in your own classroom or another classroom.
- Send the student to the principal's office. As a last resort, direct the student to leave the class and report to the appropriate principal for discipline.

There are consequences to taking formal disciplinary action. For one thing, it brings attention to the fact that there was a problem you couldn't handle yourself. Although you are allowed some latitude in this regard as a new teacher, you don't want to send students out of your classroom on a regular basis, as doing this will give the impression that you haven't established control over your class.

BE VISIBLE AND AVAILABLE TO ALL STUDENTS

Many students spend more quality time with their teachers in any given day than they do with their own parents. With so many parents working—and some working more than one job—students today often seek out a teacher to talk to before or after school, especially when something is bothering them. You never know when a student will approach you with, "Can I talk to you for a minute?" It will usually be more than a minute, and you never know what the subject will be. Frequently, students approach when no one else is around, which means at the end of the day when you are ready to go home. Here are just a few examples of the kinds of concerns that students may bring to you:

My dad took off, and we don't know when he's coming back. My mom and I really miss him.

My best friend doesn't like me anymore. She likes the new girl, and they won't let me play with them.

I don't want to go to my special class. The other kids make fun of me. Can I stay here during math?

In each of these examples, students are reaching out to you. More than asking for advice or counseling, they are saying that they trust you. You are one of the few adults in their lives in whom they trust enough to confide their most pressing problems, their most confusing struggles.

> "They talk with us. They help us work through our problems and give us time to understand the situation and make the decisions."
>
> —Madison, age 11, Grade 5

Your job is *not* to solve their problems, which you have little time for anyway. You cannot serve as their counselor, for which you have little preparation. Instead, you use your relationships with students to be a good listener, to support them, and to encourage them to make sound decisions. You will be amazed what you can do for students simply by connecting with them, letting them know that you honestly care.

LISTEN MORE AND TALK LESS

In connecting with students, your primary role is as a listener, not a talker, and *especially* not an advice giver. In fact, in some instances, giving advice to students is about the worst thing you can do. If things don't work out, they will blame you for the rest of their lives.

Even worse, if the advice you offer *does* work out well, you have taught them to depend on you (or other adults) in the future. You have reinforced the idea that they don't know what's best for themselves, that they can't make their own decisions.

Rather than telling students what to do with their lives—and you certainly will have some rather strong opinions on the issues that concern them—you should concentrate on building a strong connection in which they feel heard and understood by you. There are certain skills used by counselors, called "active listening" skills, that you may want to explore when you have the time. Essentially, these skills help you to communicate your interest and then reflect back what you've heard in such a way that the other person can work out the problem. Here are some tips for listening well:

Clear your mind of all distractions. Start by taking a deep breath to transition from what you were doing to being receptive to what the student has to say. Give the student your undivided attention. This may be more difficult than it sounds, as you must turn away from what you were doing and look directly at the student. Resist the temptation to look over the student's shoulder to see who is walking by your room. Your body language will reflect your concern and level of focus on the student. Likewise, observe the body language of the student. Is it consistent or inconsistent with what the student is saying?

Listen without interrupting. Allow the student to speak, explaining the thoughts and emotions being experienced. Resist the urge to interrupt.

Ask clarifying questions. If you have to ask a question (and often they are unnecessary), ask for clarification or elaboration. The best questions are "open" rather than "closed," meaning that they sound less interrogative and more expansive. Compare, for instance, the difference between the following conversations:

Student: "My friends won't let me join their group. They say I'm not like them."

Teacher: "Do they listen to you when you ask to join them?"

Student: "No."

Teacher: "Do you think they have a real reason or just something they made up?"

Student: "I don't know."

In this series of "closed" questions, the teacher asks things that can be answered by single word responses, closing off deeper communication. This style is quite different from the one exhibited in this alternative conversation:

Student: "My friends won't let me join their group. They say I'm not like them."

Teacher: "What has happened in the past when you try to ask to join them?"

Student: "They just ignore me or tell me to go away. It's like they don't even care what I think or how I feel."

Teacher: "How can I help?"

You can see from this example that, by asking a more open question, the teacher allows the exploration of the situation to continue and to include other areas of concern to the student. Open questions give you more detailed information about student problems and how you can help. We are not saying, by the way, that you should even ask such questions in the limited time you have. But if you must ask questions, phrase them in such a way that they elicit more than one-word answers. This generally means asking "What?" or "How?" rather than "Do you . . . ?"

And now, a brief "time out" for a quiz:

Why should you not ask "why" questions?

Your answer: "I don't know."

That's correct. Most of the time, when you ask someone "Why?" especially a child, the person will respond with "I don't know."

"Why do you keep throwing away your homework?"

"I don't know."

"Why do you keep saying you don't know?"

"I don't know."

You get the point.

Summarize what you understand. The best way to let students know that they have been heard and understood is *not* to say, "I understand." This is not only a simplistic response but one unlikely to be believed. The best way to show that you have listened carefully to someone, and understood not only the surface message but also the deeper feelings and thoughts they are expressing, is to reflect back what you have heard. Reflecting back takes considerable study and practice, but at its basic level, it goes something like this:

Student: "My friends won't let me join their group at recess."

Teacher: "I can see that you are a little confused. Tell me what you would like to have happen."

Student: "That we all play together."

Teacher: "Tell me what you can ask your friends next time."

Student: "May I play with you?"

Teacher: "Tell me what you will say if they will not let you join them."

Student: "Why can't I play? Why can't we all be friends?"

Teacher: "Do that, and see if it works. It sounds like you have a plan."

From this brief conversation, you can see how carefully this teacher is listening. She is not asking questions (not one!) but simply listening and observing the student, decoding the messages that are being communicated, and reflecting back what she understands. The beauty of this sort of approach is that, even if your reflections are not accurate, the student will correct the inaccuracy, and this, too, leads to deeper exploration:

Student: "I asked my friends if I could play with them, and they said no."

Teacher: "I know you don't like telling me because I can't make them let you play with them."

Student: "No, that's not it at all. I wanted you to know what they said. But, I guess I could try some other kids instead of giving up like I usually do."

It is beyond the scope of this chapter or book to teach you all (or even most) of what you need to get started in connecting with your students in this way. But there are other resources available (Kottler & Kottler, 2000) that can introduce you to these methods, as well as courses and workshops that you might attend at a later time. For now, we just want you to understand that connecting with students is not just about your best intentions but also about your skills, and these you can develop much further.

Your ongoing relationships with students, rather than any specific guidance you offer, will make the greatest difference. You don't have the time or the preparation to do any real counseling—besides, there are professionals in your school who have been specifically trained for that work. But within short periods of time, you can help your students feel supported and understood. At times, you can even encourage them to work toward small, realistic, incremental goals that are in the directions they would like to go. More than anything else, however, just try to make strong connections. You will be amazed how healing a supportive relationship can be.

Many students just need attention—to know someone is paying attention to them and cares about them. Make appropriate referrals to the school counselor or other professionals when a student could profit from such help. If convenient, you can offer to go with the student to introduce him or her to the professional. Look carefully for signs of severe distress; if a student does seem to be in danger of harm or abuse, you must report it to authorities.

SERVE AS MEDIATOR RATHER THAN PROBLEM SOLVER

In elementary schools, students encounter their greatest challenges in getting along with others and learning to share. In the classroom, children must share you, equipment, supplies, everything, with 25 or

30 other students. So your primary task is to help your students to grow into mature thinkers and problem solvers. You want them to become more aware of the world around them and to make wise decisions. You could tell them what to do quickly. That certainly would save time and energy. However, that is not your goal. You want to show your students how to listen, consider options, weigh the risks and benefits, and reach a decision on their own. The decision may not match the one you would choose for them, but it may be the best decision for them at that time.

When you serve as mediator, remember to guide students carefully by slowing down the decision-making process. Many of your students live in families where someone tells them what to do all of the time. You are trying to establish new and different habits of mind. Your students may not make these connections easily.

Strategies from a first-year teacher . . .

> When my students want me to tell them what to do, I repeat their concerns using "I" messages and then ask them to tell me what they really want to do. They have learned quickly that I won't solve their problems for them, and now they laugh when they hear themselves start to whine for my help.

ASK STUDENTS TO WRITE AND DRAW

One of the more effective ways of getting students to communicate their feelings is to ask them to either write or draw. If you ask students to explain to you why they are misbehaving, they will tell you they don't know. The conversation tends to stop right there. The student is waiting for you to exact a punishment and get on with it, as may happen to them at home.

You cannot do this. You need to help your students understand their misbehaviors and the consequences. One approach is to ask students to write a description of what happened from their individual viewpoints. This is particularly effective when you do not see the events occur. Independently, each student writes a brief summary and gives the paper to you to read and keep. You do not let the students read one another's papers. After you have read each paper, you decide if you want to discuss the situation with each student individually or together. Usually the students sense right from wrong and will write honest (and matching) summaries of the events. This process frequently extinguishes unwanted behaviors.

Some students may be unable to express themselves in writing. Ask these students to draw a picture of the event. Then meet with each student individually and record their words as they explain the situation. Follow the same procedures as detailed in the previous paragraph. You might want to ask students to both write a summary and draw a picture.

From another new teacher . . .

> It seemed like my students would come to me and tell me what someone else did to them. I tired of the tattling, so I made a change. The next time it happened, I asked the students to sit at their desks and write me exactly what happened, how they felt, and what they wanted me to do. Asking them to write took all the wind out of their sails. Later that week, I brought up tattling during our classroom meeting. Then we role-played various ways of coping with the situations differently and more productively.

TREAT ALL STUDENTS WITH FAIRNESS AND RESPECT

You think you're going to like all of your students and treat them all the same, but you won't. Some students seem to be nicer people and more likeable. Other students seem to be less nice and less likeable. You can dwell on all the known and unknown reasons relating to these observations, or you can strive to treat all your students with fairness, equity, and respect. This means that you approach each student as a unique individual with stronger and weaker areas, yet a whole individual who wants to show accomplishments during this year of school.

> "She is nice. She helps all the students, whoever needs help. She comes around to all desks."
>
> —Jackson, age 8, Grade 2

Each student deserves an equal chance to learn and grow. Some students will need more of your time and attention, while others seem to get by with less. Here are some guidelines:

- Be sure that every student is provided the same information. Some students may be out of the room or not listening closely when you give instructions or make announcements. See that everyone is tuned in.
- Be sure that every student is provided the same access to materials, supplies, resources, people, and so forth. If you distribute anything, from objects to turns at the chalkboard, you need to make sure that everyone gets one or can have one or has the chance to do whatever is on offer.
- Be sure that all students are provided the same or equal opportunities. This one is more difficult because you need to individualize instruction to meet student needs, and some students will be able to participate in various activities that other students cannot.
- Avoid sarcasm and facetiousness at all times. No one, regardless of age or stage in life, wants to be mocked or to endure cynicism. Saying unkind words will not endear you to anyone, and it certainly will not change anyone's behavior or attitude in a positive direction. We highly recommend that you remain kind and supportive of your students, their families, and your colleagues at all times and in all places.

UNDERSTAND STUDENT DEVELOPMENT

When we think about difficult elementary school students, we need to consider two different groups: primary (kindergarten, first, and second grade) and intermediate (third, fourth, and fifth grades). Older students usually move into middle school or junior high school configurations around sixth grade although middle school may begin as early as fourth grade in some school districts. We distinguish between the primary and intermediate age groups because their behaviors and misbehaviors, along with their reasoning, differ greatly.

Today's primary students may or may not have been exposed to many rules in their lives. Some parents of young children tend to allow their children a great amount of freedom and choice, probably more than you experienced or thought you experienced as a youngster. Some parents or child keepers often tell the children when it is time to do something and supply them with the necessary equipment at that moment. As a result, children may not develop the ability to think independently, to be responsible, or to relate their actions to consequences. Often young children do not know what they have done wrong or how to do something correctly the next time. Children may misbehave and be told that the other parent will punish them when that parent gets home. This punishment may happen many hours later, long after the child can connect the two events.

However, this is not the situation found in most primary classrooms. Primary students are given a multitude of instructions regulating their academic, social, and physical interactions. Young students may forget or become distracted easily. Teachers become frustrated; students are punished and become difficult. Students may cry, cover their heads, hide, wet themselves, take items away from another student, hit another student, or speak harshly to adults. Primary students want to please adults, but, more so, they want to get their own way. They have not matured or been helped to understand that rules are made for their own good and that cooperating with others benefits everyone.

Intermediate students and their behaviors cover a broader base. Younger ones may display self-centeredness and immaturity by crying and hiding. However, more likely, they will hurt others either physically or verbally when they do not get their way. By the intermediate ages, students start to imitate the misbehaviors they see in older children, among adults, on television, and in movies. They say words that they hear other children and young adults spout hostilely, although the words may be inappropriate and unacceptable. The children may not understand the words and their meanings. Although adults play a strong role in their lives, the older, intermediate students want the acceptance and approval of their peers.

Some intermediate students are starting to realize that rules are made for their own good and that cooperating with others benefits everyone. They also are beginning to connect their actions with consequences, both positive and negative. Ultimately, they are comparing the systems used at home with the systems used at school. And this becomes more complex when your students are dividing their time between two or three homes, which happens in divorced families, with grandparent caregivers, or in day care situations, for example. The child may or may not be capable of successfully negotiating all the various expectations and outcomes.

From both age groups, the phrase you will hear most often is, "That's not fair." No matter how hard you try or how dedicated to detail you are, at least one child will perceive that you were unfair. Try to explain to the best of your ability, and then let it go. Your student may not be able to understand your logic and reasoning. Be careful. If the student detects weakness and senses vulnerability on your part, the argument will escalate uncontrollably. To maintain your composure, speak in a commanding, yet low voice while maintaining your position.

In some elementary schools, new teachers are likely to be tested and challenged by students—and often. This isn't personal; rather, it is a rite of passage. Students, particularly intermediate students, frequently just test the limits you set on their behaviors to see how far they can go, which actions will be tolerated, and which ones won't.

The good news is that your colleagues and administration know this, and they will give you some time to find your stride. You are likely to be reassured again and again by the principal and grade level team of teachers that this is normal behavior on the part of your students. And if you experience any predicaments with students you cannot handle, you should refer them immediately for disciplinary action. Most often, this means a student who

- threatens or disrespects you, publicly or privately;
- threatens or assaults another student;
- refuses to follow your instructions; or
- disrupts the class with inappropriate behaviors.

Depending on the policies of your administration and the norms of your school, few or none of these behaviors will be tolerated. Especially as a beginning teacher, you must expect (and request) support from other school personnel and from your students' parents to help you keep your classes under control and your students' behaviors within reasonable limits. It is simply not realistic for you to expect that you can handle all discipline problems yourself, even if you had the time to do so. At the same time, you must take responsibility by setting clear rules for behaviors and implementing the expectations and consequences consistently.

"Teachers need to be in control of the students, especially the mean or angry students or the ones who don't show respect."

—Curtis, age 11, Grade 5

BE AWARE OF ATTENTION DEFICITS

Among the students most often mentioned by beginning and experienced teachers alike are those who have trouble staying focused. Students who have trouble concentrating, whether formally or informally diagnosed with attention deficit disorders such as ADHD (Attention Deficit Hyperactivity Disorder), can be challenging for both the teacher and the other students in the room. The following suggestions will help you interact effectively with students who have attention deficits:

- Seat the student near you. Your physical presence will help the student to focus on what is required.
- Provide for opportunities to change tasks.
- Prioritize "misbehaviors." Address the ones that you would most like to change first.
- Give reminders as students begin an unacceptable behavior. For example, speak to the individual who begins to get out of the assigned seat.
- Help students to self-monitor their behaviors.
- Decrease distractions. You may need to put away artifacts and objects that you have collected and put on display. Even bulletin boards need to be assessed for their "busy-ness."
- Respond to repetitive questions with one-line answers. Acknowledge the student as briefly as possible and move on.
- Remind students that accuracy is as important as speed. Encourage students to spend extra time to make sure answers or responses are correct.
- Comment when desirable traits are displayed. Make sure the student gets positive feedback during the day.
- Give handshakes. Physical contact can be helpful.

- Be calm and clear. Remain composed.
- Assign classroom responsibilities. Provide for movement in the room.
- Confer with others. Work in collaboration with other teachers to develop a plan to work effectively with students who have attention deficits.

Avoid Direct Confrontation

Whenever a student appears noncompliant, uncooperative, or defiant, whatever you do, you don't want to escalate matters by making a public show of authority or force—unless it is absolutely necessary. It is far better to censure privately. Speak in a low, calm voice. Give directions firmly but avoid threats.

Speak to students rather than touch them when there is a discipline problem. Some children will react violently—not only will they shake off the gesture, but they may attempt to strike back. Try putting a hand on their desks, if you need to get their attention.

Position yourself at their level and speak to them in a quiet voice. Remember: Everyone else in the room is watching closely to see how you handle yourself. There is a show going on, and you are the main attraction. You are being tested. Your response is crucial.

Remain cool, poised, and in control of yourself. Do not become defensive. Likewise, try not to put the student in a position in which the student is embarrassed or loses face in front of peers. Behaving this way is a tough challenge, but it can be accomplished if you have established a reasonable discipline policy in the first place and are following through as expressed in the beginning of the year.

Use a Contract System

Some students respond well to a contract system. Let's say a student continues to display a particular misbehavior or set of misbehaviors. You've held a discussion, given appropriate verbal and nonverbal cues, and maybe even asked the student to write about it or assigned a time out or two. Yet, you see no change.

With a contract, you identify the undesired behaviors and state exactly how the student should replace them with desired behaviors.

State everything in positive terms. Perhaps the student consistently sharpens pencils at inappropriate times. In this situation, write on the contract, "Pat will have five sharpened pencils each day. Pat will sharpen all five pencils every day when we clean up to go home. Mr. Watson will check Pat's pencil supply before the end of the day. When Pat has five sharpened pencils, Pat will put a tally mark on a chart or receive a sticker to be placed on a special sticker chart. When Pat has earned 10 tally marks or 10 stickers, Pat will receive a 'happy gram' to take home to his parents."

Notice that the contract states all expectations and consequences positively. There are no threats or punishments, such as "If Pat does not have all pencils sharpened, Pat will be sent to time out." You can set a timer at the end of every day when students are preparing to go home to remind Pat to sharpen pencils and then check for compliance.

We suggest that you ask the student to sign the contract. Call the student's parents and discuss your plan; then send a copy home for parents to support too. It is essential that you follow through on your contract just as you do for all consequences in your classroom. Typically, you might have only one or two students who require contracts a few times each school year.

CONTACT SPECIALISTS FOR ASSISTANCE

Many elementary schools have a school counselor or school psychologist either in the school or shared among several schools. These people are here to help you. Make an appointment with a specialist to discuss the effectiveness of your discipline plan or of your interactions with a particular student or group of students. If these students receive special services, the school counselor or school psychologist will be familiar with them and can share some information about their families and offer ideas that have been successful in the past.

You also can talk about your interaction styles and explore strategies that could help you improve. Perhaps you want to invite the school counselor or school psychologist to come into your classroom and observe you in action. This observation can be conducted in a way that is both nonthreatening and revealing. You might welcome having another adult in your classroom to shed some light on situations that you are beginning to sense are out of control.

SEEK WAYS TO ENSURE SUCCESS ...

Relationships with your students will grow and develop as time goes on. As you build a sense of trust and community in the classroom, students will bring their hopes, dreams, concerns, and needs to you before, during, and after school. They may share their personal and intimate stories. These interactions are meaningful and significant because you play a central role in these children's lives.

Students with difficult behaviors demand extra attention, so you must find ways to ensure success for them and you. If you are spending your whole day redirecting energies and enforcing consequences, talk with your mentor, colleagues, or principals. Please know that all first-year teachers feel challenged by their students' misbehaviors regardless of how they act. We think you will look back on this first year and smile at both your great insights and some of your silly errors. Learn from both, and make your classroom enjoyable for everyone!

Suggested Activities

1. With a partner, practice active listening. Take turns discussing an issue that each feels is important.

2. Identify the issues that you anticipate might come up in conversation with students. Develop possible responses that are nonjudgmental, equitable, and accepting.

3. With a partner, discuss the emotional, psychological, and social changes that occur as students progress from primary to intermediate grades and how teachers adapt to the different levels.

4. Ask a principal or counselor about the most common discipline problems seen in your school. Ask these individuals how they think the problems could be avoided or solved.

CHAPTER TWELVE

Communicating With Parents[1]

A s you organize your classroom and prepare your curriculum, you probably are concentrating on what will be going on primarily between you and your students. You will achieve much greater success in your interactions with students with the support and participation of your students' parents (Epstein, Sanders, Simon, Salinas, Jansorn, & Van Voohis, 2002). In elementary schools, many parents want to be informed of and involved in everything you're planning and doing. Parents of young children have been looking forward to sending their little ones to school for many years and to reliving some of their own happy elementary school year memories through their children. Many parents of children in every grade level want to volunteer in the classrooms, go on field trips, participate in the school festivals, and so forth. Elementary schools offer children and their parents a stable sense of community that stays with them throughout their lives.

SMILE AND WELCOME PARENTS

From the moment you arrive, you want to establish a warm welcome to all of your students' parents, but these opportunities will not

---

[1]Throughout this chapter, we use the term "parent" to mean parents, guardians, and all the adult caregivers in a child's life.

happen all at once or in the same way with each family. Some parents will drop by the school and your classroom before the school year starts to meet you privately and individually. They are eager to know who will be spending so much time with their children, and they want to peek into the classroom. Likewise, they may want to share important information with you about their child's learning styles and needs, social interactions, medical treatments, before- and afterschool care, legal arrangements, and so forth. Grab your notebook and take notes. Later, you can enter the information in the student's personal folder and check information with appropriate sources, such as the nurse or principal.

When parents and their children arrive before the school year begins, smile and thank everyone for coming to see you. Tell them how pleased you are to be a part of this particular school and community! Here's one secret from veteran teachers: stay neutral and don't talk too much about things to come. If you talk about upcoming activities or expectations, the students and their parents will share information in the neighborhood, and you might start something you did not anticipate. If you know when Open House or Back-to-School Night will be held, give the date to the parents. Then, on the first day of school, you can tell all of your students at once about everything with well-prepared details.

There are limitless ways of communicating with parents. As we mentioned in Chapter 4, you can begin by writing a letter to send home with students on the first day of school. Your letter might accompany other handouts from the classroom, grade level, or school. Some schools want parents to sign several documents. These documents are returned to the school and kept on file to show that both the students and the parents are aware of particular policies and regulations. Focus your students' attention on any papers that need to be shared with parents and returned to school immediately, especially papers requiring parents' signatures. (You may need to reward students with a sticker for returning papers. This will insure a greater return rate and fewer follow up notes and telephone calls later in the week.)

Another way to reach out to parents is to write about the classroom in a weekly letter that you send to your students and their families. Summarize some of the learning highlights as well as the social events of the week. Include reminders to students and parents, such as assignments to be completed outside of school, upcoming academic or school activities, and items that need to be brought to school. Write your letter on the computer, adding comments during the week. Make copies on Fridays to send home in students' weekly folders or envelopes.

Your school may produce a schoolwide newsletter every month or quarter. By submitting articles that you or one of your students have written, you let families know what is going on in your classroom or within your grade level team. Or, create your own class newsletter. Software programs, such as Publisher, make this an easy project. When you create a classroom newsletter, students are more aware of what they have been doing, why they were doing these things, and who was involved.

BE AVAILABLE FOR PARENTS BEFORE AND AFTER SCHOOL

Although you will meet many parents before or on the first day of school, most of these interactions are simply polite introductions. You probably won't remember the name and face of every parent you've met, and you won't have met them all. Be prepared for parents to drop by before and after school at any time. If the time is not convenient, schedule an appointment to meet with them at a later date.

As we mentioned, parents are curious about you. From the first day of school, their children have been talking about you nonstop. They are repeating your instructions and imitating you when they play school. Parents start developing an image of you right away. Imitation is a form of flattery; however, here's a little secret: your students will repeat selected portions of the school day. Their selections may both amuse and confuse their parents. Some parents will want to know more, so they can understand and support your expectations.

As the school year progresses, fewer parents will drop by unannounced. More likely, they will send a note, e-mail, or call you on the telephone requesting to see you. They may want to get more information about an assignment, question you about opportunities for their children, seek clarification about a particular social interaction among some students, or share some changes occurring in their family dynamics. If possible, ask the purpose of the meeting when they call or when you call them to confirm their written request. You can also ask whether it is appropriate for the student to join the meeting. Often, the student will provide the necessary information for clarification. Following is a secret from another teacher on talking to parents when their children are present.

From one teacher . . .

Sometimes, parents would drop by before or after school and bring both the student from my classroom and smaller preschool age children with them. I liked to have an activity ready for the student and younger siblings to do while I talked to the parents. It is difficult to talk with parents while they are supervising other children. For example, I would keep some picture books appropriate for very young children handy. I would ask the student from my classroom to go over to the reading area, (sit in my special chair), and read a book aloud to the younger siblings. In this way, the parent and I could concentrate on our discussion together.

CALL EVERY PARENT WITH GOOD NEWS AND OFTEN

An easy way to establish good relationships with parents from the beginning of the school year is to call every student's parent within the first two weeks of school. By placing two to three phone calls per evening, you can contact everyone on your class list rather quickly. Tell the parent at least one positive observation about the student's behavior (such as how nice the student is to you and other students), one academic accomplishment, and how well the student completes work and tries new assignments. Ask the parent if there is anything in particular that you need to know about the child at this time. Listen carefully, and follow up with appropriate questions or comments. Then, add, "I'm looking forward to meeting you (or seeing you) at . . . ," and finish this sentence by naming a specific time and date or event, such as the Open House, Back-to-School Night, or during parent conferences. Parents will be extremely pleased and pleasantly surprised that you took the time to call and that you care about their child. This is a plus for you and the school!

You might want to repeat calling all parents with positive comments at another time or two during the school year. Target January and April. These calls will not only make a wonderful impression but also keep communication ongoing.

PREPARE EARLY FOR OPEN HOUSE

Most schools hold an Open House or a Back-to-School Night for parents to meet the teachers during the first month of school. These events are scheduled early in the school year to initiate communication and collaboration as soon as possible and to avoid turning the event into a time for parent-teacher conferences. Generally, parents gather in the gymnasium for comments from the principal and an introduction of faculty and staff. Then parents visit the individual classrooms. At some schools, the students are invited or expected to attend with their parents. During this time, teachers introduce themselves, describe the content of the class, review the grading policy, and perhaps show examples of projects. Explain how parents can reach you, too. It's worth your while to spend a little time making your room attractive for this event. Let your students help decorate the room, and place some of their favorite papers on their desks.

Secret from a veteran teacher . . .

> Since parents would be attending with their children, especially preschool children, I would remove all of the chalk, erasers, pencils, crayons, scissors, game pieces, and so forth from the boards and centers. Basically, I eliminated any item that I thought a preschooler might use to write on the walls or that might be harmful to the child. I knew that parents would be focused on listening to the teacher's presentation and meeting other parents. Storing these items out of sight would benefit everyone.

Sometimes parents will ask questions or make suggestions to which you are not prepared to respond. A gracious way to handle such a situation is to thank them for bringing the idea to your attention, and go on. As there is no time allotted for individual attention or conversation regarding a specific concern or student in this format, a private conference can be suggested for a later date. Other helpful hints include the following:

- Practice what you are going to say aloud for timing—the allotted time may seem long for some of you, but will go by quickly for others.
- Distribute a handout with pertinent information about your class. Because the time goes so quickly, this handout will keep you on task and be a reminder for parents, as sometimes they forget what they hear.
- Pass around a "sign-in sheet" that indicates student's name and parent(s)/guardian(s)' names. (Remember, the last names can be different.) Inform your audience as to how they can get in touch with you and when and how they might expect a response.

- Pass around a conference time preference sheet. Some elementary schools schedule conferences during the afternoon and evening. You can gather feedback from the parents at Open House to help you schedule appointments for the first parent-teacher conferences (traditionally held in October or November).
- Prepare a PowerPoint presentation. Parents will see firsthand how technology is being integrated into their child's education.

The principal will help teachers manage and end the evening. Typically, announcements will guide parents to all of their children's classrooms in a timely manner. They might be asked to go to Grades K–2 at one time and Grades 3–5 at another time, allowing them ample time to visit with two teachers. Then an announcement will thank parents for spending the evening in their children's classrooms and tell teachers that they may leave within 10–15 minutes. This last announcement prompts everyone to wind up their conversations and leave together to maintain safety and security.

ASK FOR AND APPRECIATE PARENT VOLUNTEERS

Begin asking for parent volunteers when you first meet parents, in your first day of school letter, and again at Back-to-School Night. Prepare a form asking for the volunteer's name, contact information, and area(s) of interest. Many parents welcome the opportunity or expect to be involved, working in the classroom with students or helping you prepare materials. Guidance on volunteers would be a valuable topic of conversation to have with your colleagues and principal. Your school may have established specific policies regarding classroom volunteers.

Many of today's parents have other commitments and are only available on a short-term basis. These parents might chaperone a field trip, bake for a special occasion if it is permitted, or help with an evening event, such as a school carnival. Some parents are willing to donate products or supplies from home. Many parents (and grandparents!) are willing and eager to visit the classroom to be part of an audience for a performance or to judge a presentation. Many parents have an area of expertise they would be happy to share. They just need to be informed of what is needed, when, and where.

"My mom is a volunteer. She helps the teacher and goes on field trips. I like it when my mom is there."

—Francisco, age 9, Grade 3

Regardless of their availability, capabilities, or willingness to volunteer, parents will benefit from the information you provide about what is happening during the school day in their child's classroom—not only for their own knowledge but as tools to begin conversations with their children. Likewise, you will benefit because parents are key to helping you become a valuable and valued part of the school community.

ATTEND PARENT-TEACHER ORGANIZATION MEETINGS

Elementary schools tend to have fairly active parent-teacher organizations. Through these meetings, parents learn more about the curriculum, instruction, and assessments (specifically standardized testing) at their child's school. They also learn about personnel issues, budget concerns, and special events. Teachers are strongly encouraged to attend. As parents are the officers at these meetings, you will see them in various roles of responsibility in support of the school and the topics of local interest.

The National Parent Teacher Association (PTA) reports from its research that, when parents are involved in their child's education, the child does better academically, regardless of the socioeconomic status or ethnic/cultural background of the family, and regardless of the age of the child. Not only that, there is increased likelihood of the child displaying cooperative behavior, having positive attitudes, and completing and submitting homework on time. With parental involvement, students are more likely to have regular attendance, to graduate, and to go on to some form of postsecondary education.

The National PTA has six National Standards for Parent/Family Involvement Programs. The goals include

- improving clearer communication between parents and schools,
- providing programs to enhance parenting skills,

- increasing parent involvement in student learning,
- providing more opportunities for parent volunteering,
- increasing participation of parents in school decision making and advocacy, and
- improving closer collaboration between teachers and other community organizations.

Attending your school PTA or other parent-teacher organization meetings is an easy way to get to know parents and support the school.

SEND PROGRESS REPORTS REGULARLY

There are many different ways to keep your parents apprised of each student's progress (Chapman & King, 2004). When you send your weekly letter, you can attach a prepared report highlighting a selected subject area with a brief comment. Teachers often send notes home as assignments, particularly major projects with assessment rubrics, are completed and shared in class.

Helpful hints from another teacher . . .

> I made a four-line form. On line 1, I wrote a subject area with a major accomplishment such as Reading—Finished book report on time and earned A +. On line 2, I reported Spelling—90% and identified the missed words. On line 3, I reported Missing Work— math, page 31. On line 4, I reported overall behavior as positively as possible: Behavior—was an exemplary line leader this week— Thanks! At the start of the year, I completed the form by myself. Within a few weeks, each student would pass by my table during Center Time, and we would fill in the form quickly together.

These types of reports help parents know what is going on and the students see how they are held accountable for their academic progress and social interactions.

Your school may expect you to send specific progress reports on a predetermined schedule following a particular format. Talk with your colleagues and principal so you fully understand and anticipate how these forms are to be completed and distributed. You may be expected to copy them before you send them home; you might be required to ask parents to sign them and students to return them. Then, they may have to be filed in the students' cumulative folders kept in official locations.

Many schools provide teachers with telephones, voice mail, computers, and e-mail. Not only does this facilitate communication with parents, but it also enables teachers to record outgoing messages that include daily overviews, activities, assignments, and reminders for parents and students. Many teachers are even creating their own Web sites and posting information online.

WRITE THANK-YOU NOTES PROMPTLY

Don't forget to acknowledge contributions to your classroom. Whether parents or members of the community volunteer their time, expertise, or make a donation, it is important to send a thank-you note. Your school might have stationery printed with the school's letterhead just for this type of correspondence. Be sure to express your thanks sincerely identifying the specific gift or gesture, and send the note as soon as possible. Better yet, have the students compose the letter or send individual notes.

Elementary school parents may send personal gifts to teachers particularly around the holidays or at the end of the school year. Be prepared and plan to receive these items and, throughout the day, write personal thank-you notes. Bring your own stationery, so you are ready. Thank the student and the student's family for thinking of you at this time, and mention the item. Here's a helpful secret: give the students their notes of thanks as they leave for the day. Then, if this is the last day of school before winter break or for the year, you can gather up your gifts and not worry about sending thank-you notes through the mail during your vacation. This is a huge relief, and everyone is happy. You might also consider sending a card with short note (Happy New Year! or Have a good summer!) to each student during the school vacations.

PLAN FOR PARENT CONFERENCES

There are two kinds of parent-teacher conferences: informal, as discussed earlier, and formal. For all informal conferences, we recommend that you record the meeting in two places. First, note in your planner that the meeting or telephone call was held on a specific date at a specific time. Earlier, we suggested that you leave space in your planner for before- and afterschool activities and use a different colored pencil. Second, summarize the conversation, and place this summary in the student's personal file. Record the date, time, participants, who initiated the meeting or conversation, the highlights of the conversation, and any follow-up tasks that need to be completed and reported to the parent, student, or someone else. By keeping a running record in each student's personal file, you can track conversations quickly and easily.

Formal conferences usually occur two or three times during the school year. These 20- to 30-minute conferences frequently occur during the afternoon and into the evening, accommodating a variety of working parents' schedules. The first one is scheduled after the end of the first quarter, traditionally around October or November. Some school districts follow modified schedules, holding their first conferences earlier in the year.

Thoughts from a teacher . . .

> From my information sheet, I had a record of the siblings of my students who also attended the school along with their teacher's names. When it was time to schedule conferences, I sent notes to the teachers where my students had siblings. Then I sent notes to the parents telling them the dates and times available for conferences and asking for their preferences. I would note on the forms sent to parents with other children attending the school that the teachers would coordinate their visits if they would like us to do that. Most parents greatly appreciated our thinking ahead in this way.

The other formal conferences usually are held mid-year or later in the spring. Some of the more progressive schools have established specific purposes for each of the three conferences. The first conference is held within the first month of school, and the teacher meets with both the parent(s) and the student. Together, they identify three goals for the student to strive for during the school year and address any concerns.

During the second conference, held mid-year, the parent and teacher meet; student attendance is optional and decided by either the school or the parent. The focus is to review progress and revisit the school-year goals.

The third conference is a student-led conference during which the student shares a portfolio of accomplishments. Each student practices the presentation in front of peers before the conference.

The parents and teachers serve as the audience to see the portfolio and to ask questions. Again, revisiting the yearlong goals is key to this conference.

There may be other conferences scheduled throughout a school year. Such meetings can include a single parent or a group of people, including the student, the student's parents, other family members, a principal, a counselor, and others (school psychologist, social worker, special education teacher) who might be relevant. Including students will give them the opportunity to express their own feelings and perspectives on behavior and academic achievement.

It is important to be prepared for each conference. You may need to rearrange the furniture so there will be comfortable places for the parents and you to sit together. If you sit behind your desk, you create a symbolic barrier; sitting across a table or in front of one another is a friendlier approach. Try to find a time and place where you will not be disturbed. Post a note on your door indicating that a conference is in progress.

Create a folder for the conference in which to put assignments and examples of the student's work. You might also want to add your written descriptions of the student's behavior. Include a copy of the student's attendance record and grades as well.

The first impression you make is *very* important. Greet adults as they enter the room. Introduce yourself, if this is the first meeting. Say hello to the student if the student is present. Use people's names. As you guide the participant(s) into the room, say something positive about the student. Give the parents a chance to look around the room.

As you begin the conference, ask an open-ended question to gather information, such as, "What does Lisi say about the class when she is at home?" Use your listening skills and watch the body language. Then, review the purpose of the conference.

Identify the expectations for the grade level, and see if there are any concerns or problems. If so, suggest strategies that might help resolve the problems. Be specific as you determine the child's responsibilities, the parents' responsibilities, and your own role. Try to set a time line for what needs to be done, when, where, and how. Determine how progress will be evaluated and monitored.

In concluding the conference, invite each person to summarize his or her understanding of the conversation. Make plans for further communication. Finally, thank the parents for coming.

After the conference, you can take time to write down some notes (if you didn't do so during the meeting) to place in the student's personal file. Reflect on the conversation, and ask yourself the following questions:

- Did I give participants time to share a view?
- Did I mention positive aspects of the student's behavior and work as well as the problem areas?
- Was I prepared with samples of the student's work and examples of behavior?
- Did I keep the focus on the student and not on the school or the parent?
- Did I maintain my composure throughout the meeting, staying empathic and responsive?
- Was a specific plan developed to foster progress in the future?
- What was forgotten or neglected that I may wish to deal with in the future?

CONTACT PARENTS IMMEDIATELY WHEN CONCERNS ARISE

Although we wish that all contacts home involved reporting good news, it is far more likely that we contact parents by phone because their child is being noncompliant or difficult socially, academically, or both.

When making such contacts, be as sensitive and uncritical as possible so that parents don't become unduly defensive and uncooperative themselves. (Obviously, they will not be thrilled to hear negative reports about their child.) Emphasize that you share the same values and concerns with the parent regarding the student's welfare and education. Acknowledge, if appropriate, that this can be a difficult time between parents and children. Try to stay neutral, calm, and supportive.

If you are verbally attacked, or it is obvious the parent isn't listening, then disengage as best you can without making matters worse. Schedule a parent conference with the principal.

Basically, you are simply informing parents of what you have observed. Provide specific examples of what you have seen, mentioning a few of the student's strengths as well as specific weaknesses. Then, ask for the parents' help.

Teachers often call home when there is trouble. The student is being a pest in class, or is not turning in work, or might even be failing. The parents of many students have even become conditioned over time to associate bad news with teacher calls home, and they may have become understandably defensive. It is as if teachers are criticizing their parental competence, saying their children have turned out the way they have because the parents are limited in their knowledge and expertise.

Actually, we may think that, on occasion, and our goal is to help everyone. Many of the students we see come from homes with living situations that include poverty, unemployment, physical or sexual abuse, neglect, excessive alcohol consumption, drug abuse, little supervision, little help with homework, angry or violent behaviors among the adults, inconsistent or minimal discipline, and little or no support for excellence in school. Students in such situations experience hopelessness, despair, and a lack of positive role models. No wonder some students struggle so much.

Still, parents are the keys to any lasting change efforts we might wish to promote. They can be our best friends or our worst enemies. If parents are unsupportive, they can easily sabotage any potential their children have to succeed in school or in life. Often, what we are doing seems threatening to them or maybe incomprehensible. Even if children want to do their homework or prepare for class, they may be teased or scorned mercilessly by their siblings, parents, and friends. That is why it is so crucial that teachers do their best to connect with parents, in order to build positive relationships.

One easy way is to find a reason, almost *any* reason, to make another contact—call parents, e-mail them, or write them a note when their children do something that is a step in the right direction. Here are some examples of positive calls home you might make:

- "I've been really impressed that your daughter has come to class on time three days in a row. Whatever you're doing, it seems to be working."
- "Your son turned in a report this week, and although he needs some guidance with his punctuation and grammar, his ideas were really interesting. I just wanted to let you know that I think he's got some real potential as a writer."
- "I wanted to let you know that a new student enrolled today, and your child offered to be that student's lunch buddy. That showed some real compassion."

Look for the slightest signs of improvement in your students, any evidence at all that they are growing, learning, or changing; then positively reinforce that behavior by telling them how much you appreciate their efforts and by telling their parents. Keep the communication ongoing.

UNDERSTAND LIMITED RESPONSES FROM PARENTS

There are many reasons that some parents make limited or no response to our efforts (Cattani, 2002). For some, the problem is time or economics—work schedules prevent parents from calling or coming to the school. Many parents have limited access to a telephone during the work day, and, even if they do have access, their calls will not be private, so they are unlikely to contact the school. Some parents have small children or elderly parents for whom they must care, or parents lack transportation to come to school.

As you are aware, many parents have difficulties speaking English, or lack confidence in their language proficiency. This may also account for why they do not provide homework support. There may be cultural factors as well. In some cultures, the responsibility for education is left entirely to the teachers, for whom parents have great respect. These parents do not believe in crossing into the teacher's domain. Other parents have had negative experiences in the past when they were students or with their other children and have chosen to avoid contact if at all possible.

While it can be frustrating and disappointing when our efforts do not bring the successes we would like, we hope you will be understanding and continue to work to encourage parent and family involvement. Many schools and districts are working to implement programs to improve parental involvement.

INCLUDE FAMILIES IN ALL YOU DO . . .

We have frequently heard teachers, especially in lounges, complaining about how much time it takes to contact parents and about how limited are the results, if any, of their efforts. While a small minority of parents certainly may be unappreciative, critical, or uncooperative, most of them will be absolutely delighted that you care enough to communicate with them and elicit their help. Your students' growth and achievement will be greater when you communicate clearly and frequently with their parents. Parents are your partners; your success depends on them (Bergen, 2000).

Suggested Activities

1. With a partner, role-play several parent conference situations: introduction, progress reporting, low or minimal achievement, and misbehavior.

2. Interview several parents on their experiences with teachers at parent conferences. Explore what has been most appreciated by them.

3. Develop a lesson to teach students to make introductions presenting their family before the first evening event. This will help you know who may be coming and if parents and family members use different last names than the ones used by your students.

4. Develop a format for a weekly newsletter. Make a list of topics you might include.

CHAPTER THIRTEEN

Using a Substitute

"Why were you gone?"

"That teacher made us follow her rules."

"The principal came and read us a story yesterday."

"We made you get well cards."

"I don't want you to be absent ever again."

Students frequently make these kinds of statements to teachers returning from an absence. Elementary school students usually like their teachers very much and are protective not only of their teachers but of their classroom and procedures. From the first day of school, you have worked hard to establish a sense of community and continuity. You have developed routines and rewards that help everyone feel safe and comfortable. Your students tend to view substitute teachers as outsiders who do not understand or appreciate how things are done in their classroom.

> "They don't know anything, our schedule, anything we do; they are always late. I know we aren't going to do any work when there is a sub."
>
> —Zachary, age 10 (almost 11), Grade 5

During your first year of teaching, you will try hard not to be absent. Most new teachers are scrambling from day to day, and getting ready for a substitute presents a formidable task. However, there will come a time when you will need to be absent from school, and it may arrive sooner than you anticipate. You may become sick, be required to attend a professional development program, or need to take a personal day. In any event, when you are not going to be at school or in your classroom, special arrangements will have to be made for a substitute. Perhaps you worked with or as a substitute teacher in the past (Pelletier, 2000); now it is your turn to prepare for the substitute.

KNOW HOW TO ARRANGE SUBSTITUTE COVERAGE

The procedures for arranging a substitute vary from one district to another. In one location, you may contact the substitute yourself; in another location, you will contact a school or district assistant who makes the call; in yet a third district, you may telephone information to a Touch-Tone system. Frequently, you will have the opportunity to state a preference for a particular person to be your sub.

As soon as you know you need to be absent for a whole day or several days, contact the appropriate individuals. If you feel ill as you go to bed, set your alarm early so you can make your decision as early as possible about whether to go to work or stay home. The individuals responsible for contacting substitute teachers usually go to work around 4:00 or 5:00 AM. They have to receive teachers' messages, reference their files of appropriate and available subs, and call the substitute teachers. It may take several calls to cover every classroom. Many of you have worked as substitute teachers, so you have experienced getting those calls in the early morning.

It's handy to have the phone numbers you need easily accessible, such as in your wallet, as you may not feel well when you are placing your request for a substitute teacher or you may be in a rush. You may be on your cell phone en route to the emergency room. Be ready to give information slowly and clearly to the secretary. Form 13.1 lists information that might be requested by your school district.

Person and Telephone Number to Contact When Requesting a Substitute
Teacher's Complete Name
Teacher's Employee Identification Number
School
Grade Level
Day and Dates the Substitute Teacher Is Needed
Expected Times of Arrival and Departure
Special Information (for example, field trip—wear flat shoes and bring a sack lunch, or field day—bring gym shoes)
Information Required by Your Principal or District (see the faculty handbook)

Unfortunately, your absence may become necessary after you have arrived at school. You suddenly become ill, or a family member needs you to leave school early. Contact your school secretary or principal to help you make arrangements to leave quickly. Then, if your absence continues beyond the one day, you will follow the school procedures for day-to-day or for long-term absences. You can see the benefit of keeping vital information with you at all times.

Occasionally, you must be out of your classroom for part of the school day on school business without students. Perhaps you need to attend a meeting. You must ensure that your classroom has a certified teacher at all times. In some schools, the counselor or principal will provide temporary coverage. Or, other teachers may be asked to cover your class during their planning times. Sometimes, students are grouped in other classrooms, so one teacher can oversee two groups. If another professional provides quick coverage for you, you will want to offer the same services for other teachers in the future. School districts have incorporated various approaches for honoring teachers' contracts when these types of situations occur. You may or may not be paid for teaching two classrooms of students or giving up your planning time to cover another class.

SELECT ABSENCES JUDICIOUSLY

Teachers have approximately ten (10) days per school year during which they can be absent. In some places, you have to state exactly why you are going to be absent, e.g., illness (your own or that of a family member), death in the family, school business, or a personal reason. Most school districts have clarified who constitutes a family member and what conditions qualify as a paid absence, such as the event of illness or death. These expectations have been established to reduce excessive or needless absences among teachers.

You must consider each absence carefully. You need to stay home when you are ill; please, do not share your cold with everyone else. When you are not well, you cannot do your job well, and it places a burden on everyone. At the same time, it is easy to give yourself a "day off" to stay home and simply rest once in awhile. If you do this too frequently, you will run out of available days of absence, and you may need them later on. Some school districts have a "use them or lose them" type of policy; teachers cannot accrue or carry over unused absences from year to year. In this situation, you will want to be careful about suddenly being absent every Friday throughout the spring. School districts cannot find enough substitute teachers to cover all classes, and principals view this behavior unfavorably.

When you know you are going to be absent, we encourage you to talk with your principal. Be ready to explain how you plan to provide coverage in your classroom, and stay in contact with the substitute, the school, and your grade level team if your absence becomes extended. Your principal may offer you guidance for coping with new and unknown circumstances.

From a re-entry teacher . . .

> When my father was terminally ill, I had just begun a new teaching position. Before the school year started, I let my principal know the status of my father's condition. When my husband called the school to inform me of my father's death, the principal was the one who came to tell me and helped me make preparations to leave school.

PREPARE GENERAL GUIDELINES

In preparation for an absence, most elementary school teachers are expected to prepare several different types of notes for substitute teachers. The first type addresses general guidelines. Frequently folders are kept by the school secretary in the main office to give to substitute teachers as they check in for work. Include the following items with your general guidelines to provide brief directions for getting started:

- **Introductory overview.** Begin with the correct spelling of your name, the grade level you teach, all subjects that you teach, the typical daily schedule, and a class list for each subject that you teach. Reassure the substitute that more details are waiting in the classroom. Indicate any special needs students that the substitute teacher must know about right away or any requirements to talk with other professionals on the way to your classroom. Leave the names, room numbers, and telephone numbers of any necessary contacts in this folder.
- **Mailbox check.** Before leaving the main office, the substitute teacher should check your mailbox for any important information pertaining to that day or to any of your students. In some schools, the secretaries assist substitute teachers with this task to help them differentiate between items that need immediate attention and items that should be left for the classroom teacher.
- **School map.** It is helpful to leave a school map showing the path to your classroom. Also, indicate the nearest fire alarms, outside exits, restrooms, principal's office, cafeteria, and faculty lounge.
- **Grade level team office, colleagues, and assistants.** Direct the substitute teacher to your grade level office or planning area to meet your colleagues and teaching assistants. Here the substitute teacher may acquire more information about the day, students, and resources.
- **Location of substitute folder or notebook.** In your general guidelines, identify the location of your detailed substitute teacher folder or notebook and of the emergency procedures list or file in your classroom.
- **Special duties.** Highlight your responsibilities for bus duty, hall duty, lunchroom duty, or playground duty at a particular place and time.

- **Volunteers.** List your regularly scheduled volunteers, such as classroom parents, senior citizens, high school students, or preservice teachers. Include everyone's schedules and assigned tasks so the substitute teacher is prepared when these people come into your classroom.

INCLUDE SPECIFIC INSTRUCTIONS

Try to leave your classroom every day as if you were going to be absent the next day. If you have ever worked as a substitute teacher, you know the importance of coming into a classroom and finding everything ready and in its place with clear instructions and expectations. And, if you leave your classroom ready for a substitute every day, you have much less worry when you arrive the next day. It is a wonderful work habit to establish during your first year of teaching,

Prepare specific instructions in a substitute teacher folder or notebook to place in clear view on the side of your desk. Include copies of the following items:

- **Current class list for every class that you teach.** In some teaching assignments, you will teach all of the same students all day. In others, you will teach different students throughout the day. In this case, identify, by providing homeroom teacher's names and room numbers, where students go when they leave your class and where students come from when they enter your class.
- **The names of each student who leaves the classroom for special classes, events, or needs.** List the students' names, destinations, the length of time the students will be away, and the names of teachers responsible for the students while they are out of your classroom. This includes all special education, gifted and talented classes, speech and language classes, trips to the health office, and organization and club meetings. Explain how the student knows it is time to go and whether the student should take a pass or materials.
- **The daily schedule with exact times and locations.** Be as specific as possible about times, and allow extra time for making transitions. You may be able to take five minutes to use the restrooms prior to taking students to lunch. A substitute teacher needs to allot more time. You may want to add a note saying that

this is extra time and to leave a book or a poem to read aloud if the students get ready faster than you anticipate.

- **Different schedules for different days and how to know what type of day it is.** On some days, your class may go to music or physical education. On other days, they may go to art or the media center. On days when there is bad weather, you may have indoor recess. Leave all of these schedules and the way a substitute teacher can find out what kind of day it is going to be.
- **Current seating chart for every class that you teach.** Write the first and last names of all students. You can make small notes on the seating charts addressing special learning needs or behavioral expectations.
- **Behavioral systems.** Describe how you expect your students to act and the resulting consequences. Include the schoolwide discipline policy and your classroom expectations.
- **Emergency plans.** Leave detailed instructions and maps of all emergency plans in anticipation of fires, earthquakes, tornadoes, storms, shelter-in-place, lockdown, missing child, injury or illness, and other possible emergencies in the substitution folder and next to the main door at all times. Each of these folders must have all current class lists, school contact information, and student contact information.
- **Emergency equipment instructions.** Include instructions about where to find emergency equipment such as the intercom, telephone, first-aid kit, soap and water, the fire extinguisher, and perhaps a flashlight and other useful items.
- **Student helper chart.** Note where the student helper chart is and what each helper is expected to do. You might even have a substitute helper whose job is to fill in for any missing student helper and to assist a substitute teacher.
- **Special student needs.** Some of your students will experience additional difficulty when you are absent and their routine is changed. Leave a list of names and ways you have found helpful in assisting these students. Identify other school personnel who can assist if needed.
- **School forms.** Include blank forms. The attendance and lunch count will have to be reported. Substitutes may need to write passes for students to go to the office, nurse, cafeteria, lost and found, and the media center. They may be required to submit a report on a specific form at the end of the day.
- **Class signals**. Describe your signals for getting attention. If you have a student helper assigned to assist the substitute

teacher, the student helper can demonstrate or implement each signal.

- **Off-limits areas.** Specify to your substitute teacher any areas, such as a supply closet or a desk drawer, that you consider off limits to the substitute, to the students, or to both. State these expectations clearly in your substitute procedure folder. However, be warned that the substitute or the students may not be informed or may not follow your instructions. Be sure that confidential information and personal treasures are kept locked and safe.
- **A note of appreciation.** Thank substitute teachers for doing their best and for keeping your classroom as neat and tidy as they found it. Here's a powerful little secret: leave a special treat for your substitute, such as a granola bar. They may not know that they are going to work until the last moment and might leave their houses without eating. They may not know much about the school, students, or subject areas they are asked to substitute teach. You want your subs to do all they can to support your students and school, to teach your lessons, and to leave your classroom in good shape. Thank them!

Substitute Teacher Folder Checklist

- Current class list
- Students who leave the classroom (for special classes, events, or needs)
- Assistants who come into the classroom (to provide special help for the teacher or students)
- Daily schedule (with times and locations)
- Different schedules for different days (how to know what type of day it is)
- Current seating charts
- Emergency plans
- Emergency equipment
- Student helper chart
- Special student needs
- School forms
- Class signals
- Off-limits areas
- A note of appreciation

KEEP PROCEDURES CURRENT

Many teachers write their substitute teacher guidelines early in the school year and place them in the logical locations on their desks. They check to see that procedures for a typical day and emergencies are all in place. In some schools, teachers are required to provide the principal or grade level chair with a copy of the general guidelines along with instructions indicating where specific guidelines and procedures are kept in the classroom.

However, some teachers overlook keeping their guidelines, class lists, and procedures current. Within a few weeks and certainly after a few months, most have been modified. Teachers need to remember to update them so substitute teachers can do their jobs efficiently and effectively. If the guidelines and procedures are inaccurate, important information may be neglected, impacting students and other teachers. We strongly urge you to double check your substitute information and revise it as necessary throughout the school year.

LEAVE MEANINGFUL PLANS

To keep the educational flow going as much as possible while you are absent, try to create a meaningful experience for the students (Brophy, 1998). Select activities that are consistent with their units of learning. Write objectives that the substitute can communicate easily to the students so that everyone will know what the expectations are for each subject. The students should be informed as to what will be required of them and what they need to do to stay on task. This communication will provide for the best use of time for students as well as the substitute.

If you know you are going to be absent, you have choices. You can either expect the substitute to teach what you would be teaching if you were there, you can create a special plan just for this day, or you can leave an all-purpose lesson plan for the substitute to follow. We have found that most teachers who know they will be absent prefer their subs to teach a routine lesson.

If you want the substitute to teach a unique lesson, you will need to leave extremely detailed plans. Explain the special features and how you anticipate students will respond. You may not be able to avoid doing this. Perhaps a guest speaker is planned for a particular day. The day before this lesson, you discover that you have a fever and will need to be absent. You must provide background and instructions.

Many teachers prepare a set of "emergency" lesson plans that are ready at all times for last-minute absences. Papers for each subject area are gathered together with assignments that review prior learning. You are smart to have these materials available, so anyone can take responsibility for your classroom quickly. Using review materials allows substitute teachers to concentrate on classroom management rather than instructional procedures. Usually, both substitutes and students are able to enjoy a calm day.

Students will want to know why you are absent and how long you will be away. If you are comfortable providing this information and letting the substitute disclose it, you will prevent a barrage of questions and help reduce the anxiety level of the classroom while you are away. Furthermore, if your absence will constitute a change in the schedule, such as a new test date, presentation schedule, or project deadline, such an announcement by the substitute would be timely as well. The more the students' welfare is considered, the smoother the transitions of your absence and your return will be.

"I like it when they [substitutes] follow the teacher's rules and listen to us. The nice ones don't yell. They let you do fun stuff."

—Riley, age 9, Grade 3

GATHER ALL MATERIALS

Leave any necessary supplies in a conspicuous place, or note where they can be found. If audiovisual equipment is needed, reference this and where and how to obtain the equipment. Have everything clearly marked in your color-coded folders, and use bookmarks, so a substitute can follow your plans easily and exactly.

Check your supplies for writing on the board, constructing projects, and any other student activities. Because students will use as an excuse the fact that they don't have pencils or enough paper to do an assignment, it will make the substitute's life easier if you leave a small reserve supply. Also, to make sure the students use the class time as intended, develop an assignment that is due at the end of each lesson. This does not have to be a long writing assignment; it can be a brainstorming of ideas, a three-sentence summary, a picture—whatever you decide—something students will enjoy doing.

MEET AVAILABLE SUBSTITUTE TEACHERS

In most districts, there will be substitutes who are well acquainted with the faculty, staff, and policies of your school. They will be known by the students too. As a new teacher, you should make a point to meet these people. One opportunity to do this is in the morning at the office, when substitutes check in. You can find out a little about their backgrounds and their experience. Another chance to talk to substitutes occurs when you see them in the hallways or the classroom next door. You may also meet them at breaks or lunchtimes. Be sure to welcome all substitute teachers; you know what it feels like to be a newcomer.

ASK COLLEAGUES FOR SUGGESTIONS

Your colleagues know what works and who will do a good job. Form a partnership with your grade level colleagues so that, when they are absent, you check on their classroom and, when you are absent, they check on your classroom. This will enhance your students' time on task and the substitute teacher's effectiveness.

When your colleagues are absent, meet their substitute teachers. Ask if you can visit them in the classrooms during your planning time, so you can watch them interact with the students. Then talk with your colleagues when they return from their absences, and cross-check your observations with their reactions. They probably will share the notes they received from the substitute teachers, so you can better anticipate what you may or may not expect if you ask for a particular substitute teacher when you are absent.

We know of many grade level teams of teachers who have a list of preferred substitute teachers and home phone numbers, so they can call them in advance of anticipated absences. They pass the subs' contact information along to other teachers in their building to ensure that the substitute has steady work in their school. Everyone benefits when teachers and substitutes network collaboratively.

CREATE A RESPONSE FORM

In order to get a meaningful report on the day's activities when you are absent, consider leaving a form for the substitute to complete. You may be looking for specific information, and such topics can be included. A sample form for a general report back from a substitute is found in Form 13.2. You will want to expand the boxes to allow for input. Your district may already have a form that meets your needs.

Form 13.2 Substitute Response Form

Date	Grade
Substitute's Name	Substitute's Telephone Number
Student Absences	Student Tardies
Student Behaviors and Concerns	
Feedback on Lesson Plans	
Comments and Suggestions	

STAY REALISTIC IN YOUR EXPECTATIONS

Few substitute teachers will fulfill your expectations to your complete satisfaction, so be realistic. You can leave the most detailed notes in the world, and unanticipated events will occur. You cannot predict and prepare for everything that will happen the day you are absent.

When you return, know that you may have to spend extra time in the morning straightening the room and laying out materials. Some of your supplies will not be where they belong, and you simply need to restore the classroom so it provides a sense of comfort. Allow yourself a few days to get the students and classroom back to being your own.

BE PREPARED AND REST EASILY WHILE AWAY . . .

You are absent because you are ill, a family member needs you, or you are involved in a professional activity outside the classroom. You must be able to rest or concentrate when you are absent. Being a new teacher makes it even more challenging for you to be absent (Guillaume, 2004). However, when your classroom is organized and your materials are ready, you can leave the building more comfortably. It is not productive for you either to race to the school at 5:00 in the morning to prepare for a substitute when you need to be elsewhere or to worry all day that the substitute will not be able to make sense of your plans. Dedicate some time and take the appropriate steps well in advance of being absent to ensure that your classroom and your students can and will continue on without you.

Suggested Activities

1. With a partner, share lesson plans you have written for review and critique. Discuss how to improve any areas that need further clarification.

2. Ask students what they like and dislike about substitute teachers.

3. Interview substitute teachers as to what their favorite classroom teachers have done to facilitate their best experiences in the classroom.

4. Talk to teachers at different grade levels for their advice on preparing for substitutes. Seek suggestions for activities that, in their opinion, substitutes have been able to implement effectively.

FOURTEEN

Getting Involved With the School

Y ou became an elementary school teacher for several worthy and wonderful reasons. You like children, and you want to work with young learners. You probably also like elementary school environments, and you want to become involved in the assortment of activities that happen at most elementary schools. Activities include academic and social events as part of the school's governance, curriculum, arts, music, sports, fundraising, and so forth. Most people have happy memories of their elementary school years and of the many events held at their schools. Now, as a teacher, you will find many ways to get involved at your elementary school, to thoroughly enjoy your work as a professional, and to recreate those memories for your students (Cattani, 2002).

ATTEND ALL FACULTY MEETINGS

Every school holds regularly scheduled faculty meetings. Faculty meetings may be held every week, every two weeks, or just once a month. Sometimes, they occur with little notice due to the need for immediate faculty feedback, quick decision making, or responses to emergency situations. Meetings may be held in the morning before school or late in the afternoon after school dismissal. At the beginning of the school year, the schedule of regular faculty meetings will be announced. Write these immediately in your calendar and in your planning book in the far left-hand column following your color coding system or some other signaling scheme.

Many elementary schools hold their faculty meetings in the mornings before school begins. Since elementary schools tend to start around 9:00 AM, the hour before school begins gives faculty time to hold meetings. Principals often use the time before school to conduct school business. Sometimes, teachers are asked to come earlier than usual for faculty meetings, so there will be time for all concerns to be addressed. Please take note of the starting time of your faculty meetings.

It's a good idea to arrive at school about 30 minutes prior to the start of the faculty meeting, so you have time to get ready for the day. Leave a note on your door saying that you are attending the school-wide faculty meeting, so parents who stop by your classroom will not wait, thinking you will be right back. Also, leave an opening activity with directions written on the board. A self-directed activity can be a lifesaver if your students need to come into the classroom before you return, perhaps because of inclement weather or because you are unavoidably detained after the faculty meeting. If you use daily openers, sometimes called a "sponge" or "bellringer" activity regularly, then your students will know what do to when you are not there to instruct them. When you return to the classroom, everyone will be calm and engaged in a meaningful task.

You should arrive at the faculty meeting with your calendar and planner, a notepad, and a pen and a pencil and a highlighter (yes . . . take one of each!). Usually, grade level colleagues sit together. At the faculty meetings, you will learn everything going on around the school. Principals will make a multitude of announcements, such as both temporary and permanent changes in personnel, classrooms, and schedules. They will talk about policies and issues, then possibly ask for faculty opinion and feedback. Various individuals will conduct discussions about curriculum and assessment, particularly textbook adoptions and educational inservices as well as standardized testing schedules, results, and recommendations. Committee representatives may give reports, and, usually, someone shares upcoming school and social events, asking for volunteers to help.

If you have questions or concerns, jot them down on your notepad, and address them quietly with your mentor, teammates, or the principal at another time. Often, a new teacher's questions or concerns need to be discussed individually or in greater depth than is appropriate during a fast-moving faculty meeting designed for the whole school.

During the faculty meeting, you will be given handouts that you should add to your notebook. If necessary, use a three-hole punch, and write the date and follow-up notes on the handout. You need to keep a record of all papers that are given to you throughout the school year.

Transfer dates into your calendar and/or planner; highlight tasks that need either your immediate or long-range attention, again marking the due dates into your planner. It is likely that the faculty meeting will end just as your students are arriving at school. You will have only a few minutes to use the restroom and get yourself to your assigned position (classroom, bus duty, hall duty, and so forth). Your students are waiting for you. Parents may be there too. You want to enter your classroom calm and collected.

INTERACT WITH YOUR TEAM

You will be assigned to a team of teachers according to grade level, subject or content areas, or attendance tracks, and here you have several wonderful opportunities to get creative ideas and emotional support. Most likely, you get to work with a group of teachers who will do everything they can to help you become an active part of the school and achieve success. There is much to do, and they can use your help.

Teams of teachers tend to be combinations of vastly different kinds of individuals. This diversity will serve you well. You can identify with each member of your team in different ways. As you become more acquainted with each member of your team, you'll begin to recognize that each one has not only an expertise in the classroom but also a special gift for working with members of the school community. One member of your team may work well with parents and volunteers while another may be active collaborating with other teachers on special projects. Other members may like to serve on particular committees related to curriculum changes or textbook adoptions. You will start to see the members of your team in many different capacities outside of the classroom.

Although we encourage you to take advantage of your team's gifts and talents, we want to warn you about taking advantage of their time and generosity. Most likely, your team will offer to assist you, especially at the start of the school year. Quickly, you need to demonstrate increasing levels of independence. You want to be able to give back to your team members as much as they have given to you by sharing and developing your strengths.

You also want to monitor how much of the time you dominate with your concerns. Relationships with your students, their parents, other colleagues, and principals will begin to build. Some may become more challenging than you initially anticipated, or you may feel poorly equipped to handle them easily. We want you to seek guidance from your colleagues. Just be careful not to burden your colleagues with your sense of concern.

VOLUNTEER TO SERVE ON COMMITTEES

In most elementary schools, you will be asked and expected to serve on a variety of committees. Some committees will schedule meetings that convene regularly and frequently, just like the schoolwide faculty meeting. Other committees will meet for a short amount of time, less frequently, or as needed. Explore the array of committees, what they do, which ones you are obligated to serve on, which ones are optional, and where you want to invest your energies.

One committee that you are required to attend each time is your formal grade level meeting. We say *formal* meeting because, most likely, you will talk with your grade level colleagues frequently, maybe several times every day. However, the *formal* grade level meeting may be held weekly, with all grade levels holding their grade level meetings on the same day at the same time. When schools set a specific time for grade level meetings, the principal can find and communicate with individual grade level teams easily.

If one day of the week is dedicated to schoolwide faculty meetings and a second day of the week is dedicated to grade level team meetings, a third day of the week may be dedicated to curricular meetings. Most elementary schools organize committees around curriculum, such as language arts, math, science, social studies, technology, and assessment and testing. Other areas of interest are school administration, diversity, safety, outdoor education, community volunteers, special events, schedules, and budgets.

Schools will address different academic and social issues depending on each school's particular location and situation. Usually, all teachers are expected to serve on at least one curricular committee and one noncurricular committee to represent and report program ideas and changes to their grade level team of teachers.

Monitor your time carefully. It is easy to jump in eagerly at the beginning of the year and volunteer for many responsibilities only to discover that your committees are quite time consuming or require more attention than you are able to give.

ASSIST WITH PROJECTS AND PRESENTATIONS

In addition to regularly held committee meetings, every elementary school has special projects and presentations just for faculty. These include endeavors such as textbook adoptions, resource reviews, library/media selections, technology equipment upgrades, test data analysis, and best practices related to curriculum, instructional strategies, assessment techniques, multicultural education, special education, and other topics.

Commonly called ad hoc committees, these groups are either selected by the principal or composed of grade level volunteers, and their task is to examine a specific concern and to make a presentation of options and outcomes to the faculty. These committees may meet for a short amount of time, or they may be ongoing. Because new teachers sometimes can offer only limited expertise and experience, they may be protected from serving on these types of committees. If you are asked to serve or are appointed, be sure the chair of the committee understands that you are a first-year teacher, you are eager to learn, and you will contribute as best you can. Sometimes, new teachers know quite a bit about a growing concern because they recently studied a variety of concerns in their university teacher preparation courses and have observed many different schools and classrooms. The other teachers will look forward to your sharing of knowledge and insights.

HELP WITH CURRICULAR WRITING

One significant way to get involved with your school is to serve on a curricular writing committee. These committees may be unique to your school, especially in small districts with only one elementary school. Curricular writing committees may have members representing all the elementary schools if there are only a few elementary schools in a district. In larger school districts, committee members may come from and meet in one area of the district. You may be selected to serve on a curricular writing committee particularly if you have either voiced an interest in a particular area of the curriculum or demonstrated expertise in your classroom. Frequently, first-year teachers bring new knowledge and skills along with academic enthusiasm that benefit curricular writing committees.

Curricular writing meetings may be held during the school day or after school for several hours over the course of several months. In the latter case, you may experience conflicts with family obligations, your induction program, or other commitments. And, most likely, you will be expected to contribute additional efforts to the curricular writing outside of the committee meetings. You will probably serve as a liaison with your school administrators and faculty. There may be literature to read, other schools to visit, and presentations to give at faculty meetings to get colleagues' feedback. Talk with your mentor or grade level team of teachers to find out more.

There will be plenty of opportunities to help with curricular writing throughout your years in the classroom. Regardless of your level of participation during your first year, be aware of what these committees do, how they operate, and how you can stay informed both as a classroom teacher and as a developing professional. These committees are working for you!

PARTICIPATE IN SOCIAL EVENTS

Elementary schools have several types of social events. Faculty and staff usually have a social committee whose members collect money annually and attend to social concerns and activities. Frequently, new teachers are asked to serve on the social committee twenty dollars as a way of helping them get to know everyone quickly.

Most social committees ask faculty to give around twenty dollars a year and staff to give about ten dollars a year to the social fund. (Please remember that staff or noncertified personnel do not earn the same incomes as faculty.) Members of the social committee send cards, flowers, and gifts to individuals for illness, death, weddings, new babies, and other special events. The social committee generally determines exactly how money will be spent and publishes guidelines. Some social committees acknowledge birthdays and organize annual faculty and staff parties, such as a back-to-school barbeque, a winter holiday dinner and dance, and a spring banquet or pool party. Another common responsibility of social committees is to organize recognition for principals, secretaries, and custodians. When social committees attend to this responsibility, then you do not need to do more as an individual teacher unless you feel it is appropriate. We encourage you to let the social committee take care of this for you.

Your grade level may host social events, especially celebrations of faculty birthdays.

From one first-year teacher . . .

> Our team had a fantastic plan. Rather than everyone worrying about remembering and preparing birthday goodies to celebrate each other's birthdays, we decided that the person having the birthday was responsible for bringing the goodies. This was perfect for me; I hate it when people forget my birthday. And I don't like chocolate. I brought my own coconut cake to celebrate my day my way!

UNDERSTAND CLASSROOM PARTY POLICIES

Social events will occur with the students too. Most likely, your school or grade level has established a classroom party policy. Look for the guidelines regulating what you as well as students and their families can bring and give to students. This advice applies particularly to students' birthdays. The expectations range from no celebrations to no food or to food only within the last 15 minutes at the end of the school day. Sometimes, there is no policy at all. Some schools will not allow food that does not come packaged. You may have students who cannot participate in these types of celebrations due to their religious and personal belief systems. Or, you may have students who are not allowed to eat certain kinds of foods for religious or other reasons, such as allergies. Remind your students of any policy, and repeat it with your parents in a weekly note at the start of the school year.

Student birthdays can create another major challenge when students bring to school invitations to birthday parties that will be held outside of school. Sadly, the birthday celebrant usually does not invite everyone in your class. We suggest that, when you are revisiting the school or your own classroom birthday party policy, you remind parents not to send invitations to school with their children. You probably cannot stop students from distributing invitations at school. Students may pass out their invitations at lunch or recess when you are not there. Please know that no matter how hard you try, you cannot prevent the hurt feelings.

CONTRIBUTE TO SCHOOLWIDE ENDEAVORS

Throughout the year, many schoolwide endeavors will enable your students to contribute to their school and community. And, at all times, you want to model appropriate leadership and cooperation. If you do not agree with the endeavor, you need to find a way to express your concern privately, away from your students and the public eye. You have been hired by a principal to fulfill the expectations of that school and the district.

All kinds of schoolwide endeavors can be found in today's elementary schools. Some of these are formal, such as a schoolwide morning meeting. Other formal endeavors might include

- the order in which classes of students enter the building, go to lunch, and so forth
- best class recognitions for quietest class in the hallways, best attendance, best library book return rate, best cafeteria behavior, best recess behavior, and cleanest classroom
- student government
- safety patrols
- school stores
- paper recycling projects
- hall, recess, and playground "duties"
- detention
- compliance with emergency procedures

Throughout the school day, a series of informal endeavors occurs too. These are systems that occur based on presumed actions rather than on discussion and decisions. Some informal endeavors might include

- adjustments to schedules or personnel, particularly in relation to substitute teachers

- attendance at school plays and presentations
- cooperation and participation at assemblies

You will be amazed at all the systems that help make an elementary school run efficiently. No one can prepare you for all that lies ahead; some things you will just have to learn "on the job."

JOIN IN SPECIAL SCHOOL EVENTS

In addition to the various social events and schoolwide endeavors, your school will hold several special events each year.

Fundraisers. Frequently, parent-teacher organizations identify several fundraisers to be conducted throughout the year. Your students may be asked to sell items, such as candy, wrapping paper, or magazines, in the neighborhood and at their parents' employment, or they may be asked to help with an event at school, such as a carnival, dinner/dance, or car wash. Fundraisers require you to help promote enthusiasm in your classroom sometimes initiated by a rousing assembly. Then you might be responsible for collecting money daily or upon completion of the fundraising event. If you are selling tickets to an event, you might have to ensure that the correct number of tickets is delivered to individual students. If you are selling goods, you might have to oversee the distribution of the products to each student, and, if your students earn prizes for selling these products, you will need to see that students receive their prizes, which are typically awarded at an assembly, and can get their prizes home easily. And you do all this while maintaining constant enthusiasm and support. These fundraisers can be quite overwhelming for young students and their parents (as well as for new teachers).

If you are assisting with a booth at a carnival, you may need to allocate out-of-school time. You might be responsible for bringing the supplies or preparing items to sell at your booth. Once more, your students' involvement and the success of the fundraiser will depend on your level of commitment and excitement.

Seasonal and Spirit Day Celebrations. Your school may host annual events, such as an open house, haunted house, holiday gift shops, healthy heart fair, earth day, spirit day, and so forth. You will have to decide how much time and energy you can contribute to each event, in terms of both your planned curriculum and your time outside of school.

Plays and Presentations. Most elementary schools organize a series of plays and presentations during each school year. Some schools set a goal of letting every student participate in at least one performance per year. Plays and presentations may be the responsibility of the music teacher, the grade level team, or individual teachers. Most schools follow long established traditions. Explore these early during the school year so you can anticipate your upcoming obligations.

Curricular Fairs, Literacy Nights, Family Math, Family Geography. There are many different types of curricular school events like the ones listed here. Usually, teachers are in charge of these events, set the expectations, communicate their plans with parents, and organize the fairs completely. They may be one-night events or a series of events. Your full participation in a one-night event that involves the whole school or your grade level will likely be expected. You will help prepare academic products in your classroom during the school day and set up the displays for afternoon or evening viewing. Some events include activities for families too.

Talent Shows. Elementary schools seem to thrive on talent shows. Sometimes, these are held during the day. More often, they are held at night so parents and families can enjoy the fun too. Students love to perform for their teachers. As abilities vary, be sure to show your appreciation of all your students' talents.

Culmination or Year-end Events. At the end of the school year, an assortment of events will be held, including award ceremonies and continuation ceremonies. Frequently, these are held during the day, and your class will be expected to attend. If events are held during the evening, you will need to investigate whether you are expected to attend and if you need to be responsible for your students.

CO-SPONSOR AN AFTERSCHOOL CLUB

Some elementary schools sponsor afterschool clubs. These might include clubs related to academic interests (books, reading, writing, math, science, geography, thinking—Odyssey of the Mind), to music (singing and instrumental), to sports (gymnastics, dance, running, juggling), to foreign languages, to art (all media), to drama, and so forth. Some of the clubs may be just for fun, and some of them may include district or state competitions. Investigate the kinds of clubs already in existence at your school. You can volunteer to lead or cosponsor a club. Be sure you conduct a reality check on your time and energies if you agree to sponsor an existing club or organize a new one.

Your classroom may be used for school- and non-school-related clubs, such as scouts or religious groups. Since schools can charge a fee for outside groups, this is one way to generate extra funds. Usually, classroom teachers are asked whether an outside group can use a particular space. If you agree to let your room be used for a club, you will want to put away your desk items and learning materials in locked drawers and closets or cupboards.

School clubs provide a range of enrichment activities that allow students to pursue personal interests. Although teachers may be the primary sponsors, usually it is easy to find a parent to cosponsor the club in an elementary school. It is fun to collaborate with parents outside of school, regardless of whether the parents have children in your class.

Typically, clubs do three things. First, they have a purpose that the members devote themselves toward with intensity. Second, they connect with the community (for example, inviting guest speakers or taking field trips). Third, they usually produce a product or develop a service related to their purpose that they share or give to the school and students. For example, the art club creates a wall mural or the foreign language club performs at a school assembly.

Clubs offer students the opportunity to meet other students from many different grades. They give students the chance to experience leadership in small settings that focus on a topic of their choice. Clubs also provide students with opportunities to perform service to the school and community. School clubs also provide a number of social opportunities for students. With adult supervision, students have the opportunity to interact with their peers and engage in new experiences.

Your role as the sponsor or adviser to a club is to keep the students on task, provide some organizational skills and references, and help students with their planning. Meanwhile, you have the chance to get to know students in a more informal way. As a result of your efforts, you will witness both the difference you make in the lives of the students for whom you serve as a resource and your contribution to the maturation process of the students you are mentoring.

"It was pretty fun, and you got to learn new things that you never learned in chess. You got to play some really good players you never played before, and you got better and better each time."

—Alex, age 8, Grade 2

DEMONSTRATE SUPPORT OF ACTIVITIES

Elementary schools incorporate many different activities that may involve the whole school, a few classes, or just a few students. These activities may be long term or short term. You may feel that they align with your curriculum and instruction quite well and that your students will want to get totally involved. Or, you may feel that these special activities are something you want to do quickly with a minimal effort that produces the least amount of interruption to your classroom. Our guess is you will experience both of these reactions to the plethora of special activities that come your way during your first year of teaching.

Again, you want to demonstrate interest and support. You want your colleagues, particularly your school principals, to see you as a solid team player. More important, you are always a role model to your students. You want to show them that you are flexible and resilient.

More insights from a new teacher . . .

At first, I felt overwhelmed by all the interruptions that kept springing up. Just as I seemed to establish a bit of a routine in our classroom, another surprise came along. I could feel myself getting more and more irritated. Then, within the first few opening weeks of school, one of my second graders exclaimed with joy when yet another special activity came along. Suddenly I realized that all the special events and activities were far more important to the students than anything I was doing in the classroom. I could use their interest in events to inspire interest in academics. I had to be the one to lead my students.

Special activities include book fairs, visiting displays, school pictures, and school assemblies. They must be incorporated into your daily schedule, your teaching, and your letters home to parents. As mentioned before, be prepared with an activity (a quiet thinking game) to engage your students while you are waiting in line for your turn to participate. You cannot predict how quickly lines will move, and you want your students to be ready and pleasant.

BECOME PART OF THE SCHOOL COMMUNITY . . .

In this chapter, we have described many different ways for you to extend your involvement with the school and its community; however, you should not pursue all of them during your first year. This chapter was written so you would have an overview or the big picture of the various ways teachers get involved with their elementary schools. Now you can thoughtfully plan for your participation.

Your main concerns during your first year of teaching are to do the best job you can in your classroom with your students and to take care of yourself. If you find support and enjoyment by joining one or more of the activities described in this chapter, then go for it! Meanwhile, be aware of your energies, and be sure to pace yourself. You have a lifelong career ahead of you with plenty of time to get more involved (Kronowitz, 1999).

Suggested Activities

1. Review the types of committees explored in this chapter, and rank them according to which ones interest you most as a first-year teacher.

2. Ask a principal or grade level chair if you can sit in and observe various school committee meetings so you can see what they do.

3. Interview veteran teachers to see their levels of involvement in school and how they manage their time.

4. Obtain a copy of a school calendar, and note the variety of events that are scheduled throughout the year.

Reflections

If you want your students to become fearless, constructive risk takers, show them the way by how you lead your own life. If you want them to venture into the unknown, do so yourself. Share the books you have read and the ideas that excite you, the new skills you are learning, the travels that have changed your life. Talk about the issues facing the community, the state, the nation. If you would like them to be the kinds of people who are honest, truth seeking, and sincere, then be that kind of person yourself (Nieto, 2003).

BECOME THE TEACHER YOU WANT YOUR STUDENTS TO ENJOY

More than anything you say, your students will pay close attention to who you are. The image you have of the kind of teacher you wish to be can, indeed, be your reality. Much depends on how committed you remain to following through with your intentions.

One effective way to let your students know who you are outside of the classroom is to organize a time when every member of your learning community can share a special interest, a hobby, or a collection. You should participate too. This is one way students can learn more about you. Plan this activity with your students, deciding when sharing will occur (e.g., twice a week on Tuesdays and Thursdays—one person at a time), the amount of time an individual is allowed for sharing (e.g., ten minutes), the types of artifacts one can bring to illustrate one's sharing (e.g., costumes, special equipment, photographs, videos), and guidelines for the audience (e.g., touching or not touching artifacts, questions, audience stories, and so forth). We suggest you write a letter to send home with your students to their parents, so everyone is clear on the anticipated expectations.

You can develop many other types of personal connections too. Along with your students, you can share your favorite picture books, foods, customs, and so forth when you discuss these items in the curriculum. Again, these opportunities help to strengthen your learning community.

KEEP AN ALBUM

Many of you have begun a teaching portfolio or a binder showing evidence of your proficiency at meeting expectations or standards of teaching. This is a professional document for accountability and, perhaps, to be used in future interviews for employment. We suggest that you keep a more informal and personal record of your achievements in an album or scrapbook. You might even want to write yourself a letter at the beginning of each school year as you look forward to new beginnings and adventures. Then you can respond to your own letter at the end of the year as you reflect upon your discoveries and experiences. It will be fun to reread your letters later in your career or share them with a new teacher you mentor along the way.

Secrets from a first-year teacher . . .

> I started an album to highlight the moments of my first year. It was fun to make at the time, and, I came to appreciate it as a living historical document. I inserted the class photograph and wrote every child's name with the grade level and year. I added a few other photographs of our classroom and some special events. I asked a friend to take my picture, which I placed next to lists of my professional goals and accomplishments. I created a pocket to preserve some of the nice notes I received from the students and parents. My plan is to repeat this every year that I teach. I want to be able to look back as I progress through my career and see what happened in a nutshell. Maybe I can share it with a future teacher someday.

Keeping an album with a few items like the ones mentioned by this teacher will help you to remember your students and your achievements as well as to differentiate one year of teaching from another. Saving the letters of appreciation is important. Some days you will question your career choice. Reread the saved letters. You will know immediately why you became a teacher and the difference you make.

REMEMBER: IT'S A JOURNEY AND A DESTINATION . . .

Teachers who thrive in the profession are those who keep themselves fresh and energized. They keep abreast of the dynamics of their classrooms and the developments in their fields. They are constantly tinkering with their methods. They make changes in the ways they operate. They seek new ways to reach children more effectively and to help them learn about themselves, one another, and all of society.

One way to avoid boredom, burnout, and cynicism is to look for changes you can make in what you teach, how you teach, and where you teach (Kronowitz, 1999). You can change grade levels or specialties. You can go back to school to change the focus of your work. You can team teach with others, so you can learn about alternative strategies and styles. You can switch teaching assignments or schools. Or, you can stay in the same position but make significant changes in the ways you approach your students.

In spite of all the specific suggestions we have made and how hungry you are for even more detailed advice, there is a bigger picture to think about. Don't sweat the small stuff. Your main priority during your first year of teaching is to complete it successfully, with your sanity, health, and enthusiasm intact, taking pride in what you have accomplished. Without that, you won't have a second year or a third.

The best teachers and professors you ever had were able to convince you, on a primary level, that you had something important to offer others. That is your real job—to find the best that children have to offer and help them to discover this potential for themselves.

In some ways, your first year is the easiest one in the sense that you have no worries about keeping your excitement and enthusiasm at peak levels. Right now, you have something very, very precious: your own strong belief that you will be different. You will be the kind of teacher who keeps the momentum going, who continues to commit yourself to future growth, who is always learning, always reinventing yourself. You will be the kind of teacher whom students revere and admire, not just for what you know but for who you are as a human being. Your love and compassion and empathy are transparent, for anyone to see. Your students and their families know how much you care.

Everyone wants you to succeed. Take small steps, reflect upon your practices, make important connections, and look to your exciting future.

Specifically, we encourage you to find

1. a mentor, a knowledgeable other who can keep you informed and inspired (and you do the same for other teachers);

2. a peer, another new teacher to be your buddy so you can look after one another;

3. an avenue of professional development to continue your growth and knowledge about teaching, learning, and school;

4. some form of physical fitness to keep you active and fit; and

5. an outside group or interest that will get you away from school and fuel your fire.

You want your students to know and feel that they are vital members of and belong to their community of learners; we want you to know and feel that you are a vital member of and belong in your community of teachers. Soon, you will be a veteran.

You'll be amazed at what you get when you give to others. Each year of teaching will be much easier than the previous one. Sure, you'll continue to face challenges, only they'll be different and hopefully fewer. More important, you'll continue to experience more satisfaction and success. Take pride in all your accomplishments, and celebrate this year—and every year.

References and Readings

Abrams, L. M., & Madaus, G. G. (2003). The lessons of high-stakes testing. *Educational Leadership, 61*(3), 31–35.

Airasian, P. W. (2000). *Classroom assessment: Concepts and applications* (4th ed.). New York: McGraw-Hill.

American Association of University Women Educational Foundation. (1998). *Gender gaps: Where schools still fail our children.* Washington, DC: Author.

Ansalone, G., & Biafora, F. (2004). Elementary teachers' perceptions and attitudes to the educational structure of tracking. *Education, 125*(2), 249–258.

Armstrong, T. (1993). *Seven kinds of smart.* New York: Penguin Group.

Arter, J., & McTighe, J. (2001). *Scoring rubrics in the classroom: Using performance criteria for assessing and improving student performance.* Thousand Oaks, CA: Corwin Press.

Beaudoin, M. N., & Taylor, M. (2004). *Breaking the culture of bullying and disrespect, grades K–8.* Thousand Oaks, CA: Corwin Press.

Bergen, E. H. (2000). *Parents as partners in education: Families and schools working together* (5th ed.). Englewood Cliffs, NJ: Merrill/Prentice Hall.

Bevel, P. S., & Jordan, M. M. (2003). *Rethinking classroom management: Strategies for prevention, intervention, and problem solving.* Thousand Oaks, CA: Corwin Press.

Black, S. (2006). Respecting differences. *American School Board Journal, 193*(1), 34–36.

Borich, G. D. (2004). *Effective teaching methods.* Upper Saddle River, NJ: Pearson Education.

Boynton, M., & Boynton, C. (2005). *The educator's guide to preventing and solving discipline problems.* Alexandria, VA: Association for Supervision and Curriculum Development.

Brooks, J. G., & Brooks, M. G. (1999). *In search of understanding: The case for constructivist classrooms.* Englewood Cliffs, NJ: Prentice Hall.

Brophy, J. (1998). *Motivating students to learn.* New York: McGraw-Hill.

Bruner, J. S. (1977). *The process of education.* Cambridge, MA: Harvard University Press.

Canter, L. (1992). *Assertive discipline: Positive behavioral management for today's classrooms* (3rd ed.). Santa Monica, CA: Canter & Associates.

Cattani, D. H. (2002). *A classroom of her own: How new teachers develop instructional, professional, and cultural competence.* Thousand Oaks, CA: Corwin Press.

Chapman, C., & King, R. (2004). *Differentiated assessment strategies: One tool doesn't fit all.* Thousand Oaks, CA: Corwin Press.

Clay, M., & Cazden, C. (1992). A Vygotskian interpretation of reading recovery. In L. C. Moll (Ed.), *Vygotsky and education: Instructional implications and applications of socio-historical psychology* (pp. 206–222). New York: Cambridge University Press.

DeVries, R., & Zan, B. (2003). When children make rules. *Educational Leadership, 81*(1), 60–63.

Dewey, J. (1938). *Experience and education.* New York: Simon & Schuster.

Edwards, C., Gandani, L., & Forman, G. (Eds.). (1998). *The hundred languages of children: Reggio Emilia approach—advanced reflections.* United States: Ablex Publishing Corporation.

Epstein, J. L., Sanders, M. G., Simon, B. S., Salinas, K. C., Jansorn, N. R., Van Voohis, F. L. (2002). *School, family, and community partnerships: Your handbook for action* (2nd ed.). Thousand Oaks, CA: Corwin Press.

Erickson, L. H. (2002). *Concept-based curriculum and instruction: Teaching beyond the facts.* Thousand Oaks, CA: Corwin Press.

Erickson, L. H. (2000). *Stirring the head, heart, and soul: Redefining curriculum and instruction* (2nd ed.). Thousand Oaks, CA: Corwin Press.

Fay, J., & Funk, D. (1998). *Teaching with love and logic: Taking control of the classroom.* Golden, CO: Love & Logic Press.

Flannery, M. E., & Jehlen, A. (2005). Closing the gap. *NEA Today, 23*(4), 22–31.

Franek, M. (2005). Foiling cyberbullies in the new wild wild west. *Educational Leadership, 63*(4), 39–43.

Fritzberg, G. J. (2001). Less than equal: A former urban schoolteacher examines the causes of educational disadvantagement. *Urban Review, 33*(2), 107–130.

Gallavan, N. P. (2003). *What principals need to know about teaching . . . social studies.* New York: National Association of Elementary School Principals, Educational Research Services.

Gallavan, N. P. (in press). *Strengthening social studies education: Purposes, concepts and strategies for middle school teachers and students.* Columbus, OH: Prentice Hall Publishing Co.

Gardner, H. (1983). *Frames of mind.* New York: Basic Books.

Gregory, G. H., & Kuzmich, L. (2004). *Differential literacy strategies for student growth and achievement in grades K–6.* Thousand Oaks, CA: Corwin Press.

Guillaume, A. M. (2004). *K–12 Classroom teaching: A primer for new professionals* (2nd ed.). Upper Saddle River, NJ: Pearson Education.

Howard, G. (1999). *We can't teach what we don't know: White teachers, multiracial schools.* New York: Teachers College Press.

Ingersoll, R. M., & Smith, T. M. (2003). The wrong solution to the teacher shortage. *Educational Leadership, 60*(8), 30–33.

Johnson, D. W., & Johnson, R. T. (1999). Making cooperative learning work. *Theory Into Practice, 38*(2), 67–73.

Jones, F. H. (2000). *Tools for teaching.* Santa Cruz, CA: Frederic H. Jones & Associates.

Joyce, B., & Weil, M. (2003). *Models of teaching* (7th ed.). Boston: Allyn & Bacon.

Karten, T. J. (2004). *Inclusion strategies that work! Research-based methods for the classroom.* Thousand Oaks, CA: Corwin Press.

Kohn, A. (1999). *The schools our children deserve: Moving beyond traditional classrooms and "tougher standards."* Boston: Houghton Mifflin.

Kottler, E., & Kottler, J. A. (2002). *Children with limited English: Teaching strategies for the regular classroom* (2nd ed.). Thousand Oaks, CA: Corwin Press.

Kottler, J.A. & Kottler, E. (2000). *Counseling skills for teachers.* Thousand Oaks, CA: Corwin Press.

Kottler, J. A., Zehm, S. J., & Kottler, E. (2005). *On being a teacher: The human dimension* (3rd ed.). Thousand Oaks, CA: Corwin Press.

Kriete, R. (2003). Start the day with community. *Educational Leadership, 61*(1), 68–70.

Kronowitz, E. L. (1999). *Your first year of teaching and beyond.* Menlo Park, CA: Longman.

Manning, M., Manning, G., & Long, R. (1994). *Theme immersion: Inquiry-based curriculum in elementary and middle schools.* Portsmouth, NH: Heinemann.

Manning, M. L., & Bucher, K. T. (2003). *Classroom management: Models, applications, and cases.* Upper Saddle River, NJ: Pearson Education.

Marzano, R. J. (2003). *What works in schools: Translating research into action.* Alexandria, VA: Association for Supervision and Curriculum Development.

Marzano, R. J., Marzano, J. S., & Pickering, D. J. (2003). *Classroom management that works: Research-based strategies for every teacher.* Alexandria, VA: Association for Supervision and Curriculum Development.

Marzano, R. J., Pickering, D. J., & Pollack, J. E. (2001). *Classroom instruction that works: Research-based strategies for increasing student achievement.* Alexandria, VA: Association for Supervision and Curriculum Development.

Meager, J. (1996). Classroom design that works every time. *Instructor, 106,* 70–73.

Mitchell, C., & Espeland, P. (1996). *Teach to reach: Over 300 strategies, tips, and helpful hints for teachers of all grades.* Minneapolis, MN: Free Spirit Publishing.

Morse, T. E. (2004). Ensuring equality of education opportunity in the digital age. *Education and Urban Society, 36*(3), 226–279.

Nielson, L. B. (2002). *Brief references of student disabilities . . . with strategies for the classroom.* Thousand Oaks, CA: Corwin Press.

Nieto, S. (2003). *What keeps teachers going?* New York: Teachers College Press.

Nieto, S. (Ed.). (2005). *Why we teach.* New York: Teachers College Press.

Noddings, N. (1992). *The challenge to care in schools: An alternative approach to education.* New York: Teachers College Press.

Oakes, J., & Lipton, M. (2003). *Teaching to change the world* (2nd ed.). Boston: McGraw-Hill.

Oliva, P. (2004). *Developing the curriculum* (4th ed.). New York: Longman.

Oosterhof, A. (2003). *Developing and using classroom assessments.* Upper Saddle River, NJ: Pearson Education.

Pelletier, C. M. (2000). *Strategies for successful student teaching: A comprehensive guide.* Needham Heights, MA: Allyn & Bacon.

Popham, W. J. (2004). *Classroom assessment: What teachers need to know* (4th ed.). Needham Heights, MA: Allyn & Bacon.

Price, K. M., & Nelson, K. L. (2003). *Daily planning for today's classroom: A guide for writing lesson & activity plans.* Belmont, CA: Wadsworth/Thomson Learning.

Roberts, P., & Kellough, R. D. (2003). *A guide for developing interdisciplinary thematic units* (3rd ed.). Englewood Cliffs, NJ: Prentice Hall.

Robins, K. N., Lindsey, R. B., Lindsey, D. B., & Terrell, R. D. (2002). *Culturally proficient instruction: A guide for people who teach.* Thousand Oaks, CA: Corwin Press.

Rother, C. (2005). Is technology changing how you teach? *T.H.E. Journal, 33*(3), 34–36.

Sadker, M. P., & Sadker, D. M. (2005). *Teachers, schools, & society* (7th ed.). Boston: McGraw-Hill.

Schein, E. H. (1985). *Organizational culture and leadership.* San Francisco: Jossey-Bass.

Skiba, R. J., Michael, R. S., Nardo, A. C., & Peterson, R. L. (2002). The color of discipline: Sources of racial and gender disproportionality in school punishment. *Urban Review, 34*(4), 317–342.

Slavin, R. (1995). *Cooperative learning: Research, theory, and practice* (2nd ed.). Boston, MA: Allyn & Bacon.

Smith, T. E. C., Polloway, E., Patton, J., & Dowdy, C. (2006). *Teaching students with special needs in inclusive settings* (4th ed.). Boston: Pearson/Allyn & Bacon.

Spinelli, C. G. (2002). *Classroom assessment for students with special needs in inclusive settings.* Upper Saddle River, NJ: Pearson Education.

Stiggins, R. (2004). *Student-involved assessment FOR learning* (4th ed.). Upper Saddle River, NJ: Merrill Prentice Hall.

Tomlinson, C. A. (1999). *The differentiated classroom: Responding to the needs of all learners.* Alexandria, VA: Association for Supervision and Curriculum Development.

Tomlinson, C. A. (Ed.). (2004). *Differentiation for gifted and talented students.* Thousand Oaks, CA: Corwin Press.

Vygotsky, L. S. (1978). *Mind in society: The development of higher psychological processes.* Cambridge, MA: Harvard University Press.

Wentworth, N., Earle, R., & Connell, M. L. (Eds.). (2004). *Integrating information technology into the teacher education curriculum: Process and products of change.* Binghamton, NY: Haworth Press.

Wiggins, G., & McTighe, J. (2006). *Understanding by design* (Expanded 2nd ed.). Upper Saddle River, NJ: Pearson Education.

Wink, J. (2004). *Critical pedagogy: Notes from the real world* (3rd ed.). New York: Addison Wesley Longman.

Wong, H. K., & Wong, R. T. (2001). *The first days of school: How to be an effective teacher* (17th ed.). Mountain View, CA: Harry K. Wong Publications.

Zimmermann, S., & Keene, E. O. (1997). *Mosaic of thought: Teaching comprehension in a reader's workshop.* Boston: Heinemann Press.

Index